PROFIT FROM YOUR PC

by

DAVID LINTON

First published 1995
This edition (3rd impression) 1997

© David Linton

British Library Cataloguing in Publication Data. A catalogue record
for this book is available from the British Library.

ISBN 0 948035 16 1

Published by:
Rushmere Wynne Limited,
4-5 Harmill, Grovebury Road,
Leighton Buzzard, Bedfordshire LU7 8FF
Tel: 01525 853726
Fax: 01525 852037

Printed by:
Short Run Press Limited
Bittern Road,
Sowton Industrial Estate,
Exeter EX2 7LW

PROFIT FROM YOUR PC

How to use a personal computer
to buy and sell shares

by

David Linton

The VOUCHER for your *FREE Updata Profit for Windows* can be found on page 175.

Rushmere Wynne Limited
England

I dedicate this book to my parents,
who have always been very understanding and supportive.

David Linton
London
November 1995

ACKNOWLEDGEMENTS

● ●

Things usually take longer and involve more people than one expects. As a result there are a few people to thank. Ann Louise Stebbing for tolerating my initial scribblings when we were supposed to be taking a relaxing break in the Caribbean. Clare Rodgers who spent some time trying to understand my initial scribblings on technical analysis long ago and highlighting where I lost people. Nick Glydon, a highly regarded technical analyst, who proof read what was the first Updata manual a few years ago and kept me in line. His sister Sarah Howard Glydon, who is an experienced equities specialist for a leading financial information company, and knows me well enough to be very critical. Ian Rodgers who I met at a trade show and has become a mentor for the past few years. Many long telephone calls have helped me appreciate investment from a different, but learned perspective. Sophie Stanford Davis typed in illegible notes that I made when my PC and I were separated. Katie Pope for advising on many aspects of the book. My thanks are due to Dr Philip Treleavan at UCL, for allowing me to recompile his list of useful Internet addresses in Appendix One. To all the staff at Updata who really got behind me in bringing this project to fruition. The more we achieve, the more we set out to do. And finally, thanks to Tony Drury and his team at Rushmere Wynne for taking the bare bones and polishing them.

Please remember that the price of stockmarket investments and the income derived from them can go down as well as up. If you are not sure what to do when considering investing, please get professional advice. The shares quoted in this book are examples only and their inclusion should not be taken as a recommendation to buy or sell.

PREFACE

•••

In the last seven years I have spoken to several thousand investors. This process has happened at exhibitions, conferences, open days in computer stores, user group evenings, demonstrations and conversations over the telephone. Often these people have been more than twice my age. While there have been times where I have dreaded driving the length and breadth of the country to attend these meetings, I always come away feeling they have been very worthwhile.

My primary objective, as Updata's managing director, has been to try and understand both our existing customers and the mass of potential ones. The real satisfaction has come from the fact that in having these informal open discussions, I have learned a good deal about investors, markets and technology. Hopefully many of these people have also learned something as well.

I was reluctant to write this book when my publisher, Tony Drury, first approached me with the idea. I work day and night as it is. Increasingly, however, I could see there was a real need to produce what was becoming a very practiced presentation. If this book helps you to take another look at the way you invest, then I have achieved something. Hopefully others will take things a long way further, and make much more of their hard earned money.

This book has been written using:

1. A Gateway 2000 colour portable computer
2. Microsoft Windows '95
3. Microsoft Word (Word processor)
4. Updata Shares* (Graphs pasted into Word in three mouse clicks)

* Updata Invest was used for Leaders and Laggards in Chapter Nine and the short-term indicators in Chapter Twelve.

I welcome any correspondence from readers at:

Updata Software
Updata House
Old York Road
London
SW18 1TG

Fax: 0181 874 3931
E-mail: Internet: Readers@updata.co.uk
Updata World Wide Web: http://www.updata.co.uk

Contents

Introduction

• •

'I know all this has been said before, but I need to say it anyway.'

Rousseau 1712–1778

Can today's stockmarket investor afford to be without a computer? Answer - "No." This book is designed to show you why.

Where most investors go wrong

Having spoken to a large number of investors over several years there seems to be a common series of pitfalls. Much of the following has been said before, but clearly there is a need for re-emphasis.

I'm not picking enough winners

Deeper analysis of this shows people sell their good stocks too soon and hold their bad stocks too long. If you can overcome both aspects of this, you will greatly increase your investment profits.

It comes about because the traditional wisdom says 'always take a profit'. This phrase is one of the investors' biggest enemies as it focuses the mind on the successes and detracts from the losers. Maybe investors would do better to turn logic on its head and remind themselves 'always take a loss'. All you need to worry about in the first instance is your losses as they can run away negating your gains. Indeed it is perfectly possible to succeed with more losers than winners provided you minimise your losses and maximise your profits. This will be covered in more detail later but the four rules to remember are:

1. Cut losses

2. Cut losses

3. Cut losses

4. Let profits run

I do not have enough information

I am always amazed how much data investors carry on the companies and markets they invest in and how hungry they are for more. The question is how much of this data is useful information? The best investors spot things the crowd fails to see. Crowd behaviour is rapidly becoming one of the most useful subjects in studying markets and there is undoubtedly a very strong correlation between the way markets, and the crowds that invest in them, behave. Hence your strategy should be to spot things before the crowd does. Get in just before everyone else and get out accordingly and beware of bandwagons; they often crash.

It seems that most investors have too much of the wrong information, data, and not enough of the right information. Bear in mind that most of what you read in the press is already 'discounted' in the market. In fact the way the market has behaved often leads to the information in the press. We will show in the following chapters that a lot of the information you need is right in front of you if you can see it. Therefore always look for the information that the majority does not see.

I make the wrong decisions

Making good decisions results from having the right information and the confidence to act on it. People generally make bad decisions because they cannot see the wood for the trees. This clouded vision results from our inability to prioritise and reject the bulk of unimportant information around us. It is partly for this reason, after tax breaks, that some of the most successful investment funds are managed from remote havens, undistracted from the 'crowd' of the markets they invest in. Take a contrary view – if it is obvious, it is obviously wrong.

The best business people follow their instincts and not their emotions. Avoid doubt, which leads to fear. When investing take the emotion out. I will show you that you need to implement a trading system that removes emotion. Most people avoid cutting losses because they emotionally find it difficult to accept what they see as failure. One must develop an ability to spot a bad decision. Do not be afraid to say 'I got it wrong – it has turned out differently than I anticipated. The position now looks very different – I will get out – NOW!'.

My broker gives me bad tips

Brokers are brilliant at telling you what to buy and less good at telling you what to sell. I have spent a lot of time in brokers' offices and have grown concerned at hearing a range of common responses. Brokers are reluctant to ring you and tell you the stock they got you into last month has fallen further and you should get out. This follows on from the emotional fear of failure or admitting a mistake. Moreover, if you question a deteriorating position, you will be reassured that long-term it will pick up. This ignores the principle of time is money.

Some brokers are not motivated by the long-term prosperity of their clients. You need a broker who will assist you in getting out of your bad positions and into new good ones. This way both parties win. They get their commission twice and you move forward. Execution-only services now mean that you do not have to pay for advice if you choose not to. In the end you are more often best off to make your own decisions. You can outperform the market. Above all – never take a tip. Do your own research.

What should I buy?

At seminars or exhibitions I am always asked 'What should I buy?' 'Simple', I respond to a dismayed enquirer. 'Buy shares that are going up!' 'Why? Because they are going up'. We often find it difficult not knowing why something is happening, and it is when everyone knows why that we should be most cautious. How often do 'buy' recommendations fall while other shares have risen up and up for seemingly no good reason.

In fact, if the market does not know why something is rising this may imply that a privileged few have spotted something. In effect your tips will become spotting reversals, changes in price behaviour and identifying trends. This is a skill which will be developed with practice. The objective of this book is to get you started.

Selling now does not fit in with my tax planning or forthcoming dividend

While there are important aspects for investors to consider in this area, they should always be secondary to making buying or selling decisions. There is little point in holding out for a dividend if a stock is moving in a clear downward trend. Similarly, many investors appear to be most active at the end of the tax year. It is as if this is the only time they take a good look at their investments. Others who want to keep on top of their tax liability become obsessed with the idea of paying any tax and would, it seems, prefer to throw their profits away than give a percentage to the Government.

Clearly, there is a need to keep an eye on your tax liability. No one likes to find money they have not allowed for. Portfolio Management and Capital Gains Tax is covered from a software perspective in this book. While we don't cover the various calculations in any depth there are software products that do. This book does not cover the increasing array of tax breaks that are available. For those that don't keep on top of these, consult a professional who does. My main message in this book is that you can buy and sell your own shares based on your own research. You also have a very good chance of beating advisers in this area. Why? Because you will spend more time keeping on top of your investments, researching solely what is in your interest. Above all you WILL take every opportunity to cut losses.

Remember that tax considerations are secondary to your buy and sell decisions.

I can't keep on top of the market or my investments

The new breed of fund management company is starting to scan the mountain of paperwork they receive into a central system. It is now accepted that computers are as good at managing words and pictures as they are numbers. Computer power has increased rapidly, while cost has fallen dramatically. The investor with a pile of magazines, annual reports and stockbroker newsletters will find it increasingly difficult to keep up.

I was reading a copy of *Futures Magazine* on a flight to the US last year. On the inside front cover there was an advertisement with two images in a sort of *before* and *after* format. Man 'A' on the left was tearing his hair out with a pile of papers on his desk and was chained to his computer screen. Man 'B' was sitting in a golf buggy on a sunny day, nicely tanned with a smile on his face. Man 'B' had a trading system which he spent 20 minutes using first thing each day to keep on top of his trading.

The essence of this advertisement and indeed this book, is that you need to get your own methodical system in place. This should free up your time rather than making more demands on it.

At Updata we have been working on a joint venture with a company in Houston, Texas, developing an automated trading system. This tells you when to buy and sell a series of futures contracts. While I believe decisions will always be best made by the investor (otherwise systems on a mass scale could affect the market) the investor will have a greater range of tools available.

Another area where computers will become essential to the investor is that of screen based trading or on-line dealing. The International London Stock Exchange has announced that the market will ultimately move from a quote based market to an order driven market. This and rolling settlement (T + 5 = 5 day settlement) coming down to a level where order and transaction occur simultaneously means that you may offer your shares on the open market to another screen based investor who purchases them. This may not be unlike home shopping which is set to become a huge industry. Investors will communicate ideas and there will be massive private investment forums over the Internet. The possibilities are endless. So if you don't want to get left behind buy a computer and start getting to grips with what technology can do for you.

Summary

I have covered the bulk of technological issues which the private investor is set to face in the coming years. This is not an easy task as the industry is constantly changing in ways few could have predicted (not unlike the stockmarket). The key is to take on board the changes as they happen rather than resist them. At Updata our challenge is to make software much easier to use so that more people can receive the benefit previously reserved for City professionals.

As these changes occur so dramatically, I apologise in advan material which may be dated by the time you read it.

Points to Remember:

1. Cut losses

2. Cut losses

3. Cut losses

4. Let profits run

5. Discard useless information

6. Look for information the crowd fails to see.

7. Take a contrary view

8. Never take a tip

9. Sell shares that are falling

10. Buy shares that are rising

11. Buy a computer and the right software

12. Get a methodical system in place

PART ONE

Getting Your System in Place

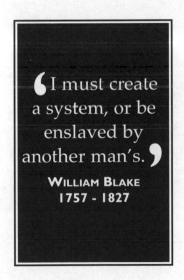

"I must create a system, or be enslaved by another man's."

WILLIAM BLAKE
1757 - 1827

CHAPTER ONE

A Methodical Approach

. . . .

Fundamentals versus Charting

There has been a long running debate between the purists of each of these camps, with each dismissing the other as misguided. It seems to be part of human nature that we feel a need to categorise ourselves rather than take on a broad range of views.

The fundamentalist will make it his business to understand the business a company is in, the people behind the company (although many private investors fail to do this) and make an in-depth analysis of the company's accounts and profit performance over previous years.

The chartist, or technical analyst is more of a technician and will spend time studying pure price movement and view a range of technical factors. With the rise of the personal computer, not to mention institutional computerised trading, this camp has become increasingly popular. Most of the larger broking houses have made it their business in recent years to have their own in-house technical analyst.

Over a period of years, the economic fundamentals of a country are what counts; for example the declining competitiveness of American industry over the past ten years has led to a long-term decline in the dollar. The same has been true for sterling over an even greater time span.

Fundamentals are less good at assessing the short-term. If a price line fails to move in a predicted direction, the fundamental analysis needs to be completely revised while the chart is constantly revising itself.

Technical factors usually account for virtually 100% of one day's trading movement. There are exceptions such as when there is a dramatic news item, for instance Iraq's invasion of Kuwait. Over a weekly basis a price line's movement is still mainly technical. After a few months movement is half technical and half fundamental. Over six months fundamentals have become more important and after a year it is nearly all fundamentals.

It is harder to act according to price changes using fundamentals and difficult to know the extent of the effect.

Investors should endeavour to place themselves somewhere between these two camps. Based on the above, you should think:

Fundamentals - Long-Term

Technical - Short-Term

I would favour a position nearer the technical camp as it lends itself more readily to the methodical approach. It is also a good distance from the crowd.

In the Introduction we mentioned that part of our strategy should be to find information that the majority of investors did not see. We will also show that much of this information is potentially right under our noses. This is certainly the case in studying the price history.

Figures versus Pictures

A trader gets a feel for the market in a way that most investors do not. They will spend their intense day assimilating figures either on a crowded trading floor or (increasingly) on a screen. Because they are immersed in their market they build an instinctive understanding of the relationship between price and value. The problem with a screen or newspaper page full of prices, is that we are unable to make good use of this data. We will show the advantage of the picture rather than the price throughout this book.

The Graph

Before we look at the relationship of price versus value, we should look at the basic concept of the graph.

We all learned from an early age the value of taking tabular data and plotting that data so that we can view it graphically. This is often an enlightening experience. Judging by the way most private investors react when they are shown graphs, this is also the case with price histories.

What does the graph represent?

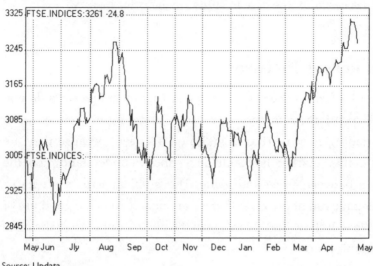

Source: Updata

My favourite interpretation of this is: 'The graph represents all the information that everyone in the market already knows about a particular stock or about the shares comprising an index.'

What you don't need to know

Whenever I am showing a graph to someone who knows a good deal about a company, as we talk through the movements, the peaks, the troughs, there is a need to justify them. This information is normally not always useful. Again it highlights our instinct to understand the cause when what we should be studying is the effect. The graph will often tell you all you need to know.

Price versus Value

It has been said that 'Markets will tell you the price of everything and the value of nothing.' Most of us relate to this adage as we frequently see the stocks we buy keep falling and the ones we sell, start rising. The harsh reality is that most securities are rarely at or near their real value. Nearly all stocks spend most of their time being either overbought or oversold.

The graph below shows a central regression line through Cable & Wireless shares over the last twelve years. This line is the mathematical average of the price movement over the period. In twelve years the shares have only crossed this line a couple of dozen times. Given this is the general trend of the share price, it seems a fair assumption that over the period this line is close to the true value of the share, yet the price of the shares was a long way from this value throughout most of the period.

Source: Updata

Fundamentals on your PC

There is a shortage of fundamentals related information for the PC available to private investors. Some of the City screen systems have company accounts, directors dealings and recent press comment on-line.

This type of information will start to appear over the coming years, either on CD-ROM, the Internet or closed user group on-line services, such as CompuServe. At Updata, we are talking to a range of media companies with the view that we must find a way of providing the private investor with this type of information on a frequent basis.

This area of data acquisition is covered further in Chapter Three, *Getting Data*. There is also an increasing amount of electronic fundamentals data available on the Internet: see Chapter Four and Appendix One.

CHAPTER TWO

Computers

● ●

Buying a computer

Advising on buying a computer is not easy. People ask us for advice every day of the week. Prices and specifications are changing all the time. You need to take the plunge sooner or later. At the time of writing, several hundred pounds would buy a system which would suit the needs of most private investors. If you don't want to walk through the minefield, spend about this much. For those who would like to consider their purchase more closely before they buy, this chapter offers some general guidelines.

Walk into a newsagents and you will see several voluminous monthly magazines dedicated to PCs and software. This doesn't make choosing a computer any easier. There are a number of different types and makes. The two main PC formats are Apple and IBM compatibles; the latter now account for more than 80% of the PC market.

Apples have traditionally been used in the design and printing end of the market although their latest range called Power PC, which is also IBM compatible, should change that. Power PC has had fabulous reviews in the PC Press. They are just starting to ship with EISA (IBM standard) expansion slots for circuit cards (ie. modems or Teletext cards) so they should be seriously considered.

IBM compatible machines are available from a large number of manufacturers including the following reputable ones: Apricot; Compaq; Dan; Dell; Elonex; Gateway; Hewlett Packard; IBM; Olivetti; Texas Instruments and Viglen.

Collecting figures and drawing graphs by hand is a time consuming exercise. While it is quite useful in understanding graph construction, it is a task that one grows tired of very quickly. This is also time better spent studying a company's fundamentals or looking more closely at graphs. It is also the kind of operation that personal computers are ideally suited to.

For those who do not have a PC, or for existing users looking to upgrade, this section covers what you need to consider.

I am frequently asked by friends and clients what computer they should buy. It is a question that has got harder to answer over the years with an increasingly wider range of choice and prices rapidly changing. *The home PC market is now the fastest growing sector in the industry.* This means that the market is maturing into a white goods mass market. There are now a number of shop and warehouse chains such as Dixons, PC World and Escom (the German manufacturer who took over the Rumbelows high street chain of shops) which sell computers.

My advice would be, if you know what you are doing buy direct from a manufacturer via a PC magazine. If you don't, then visit one or two of these shops or a specialist to get a good understanding of what you are buying.

A few general rules are:

1. Buy the top of the range rather than the bottom. A 486 DX66 is probably better value than a Pentium P60, the low end of the next level up.

2. Get as big a hard disk as you can afford. You will probably fill it up eventually no matter how big it is.

3. The more memory you have the faster your programs will run.

4. Get a CD-ROM if you can afford it, as this format is becoming the standard.

5. Choose Microsoft Windows as your operating system. It is the easiest to use and nearly all quality software packages run on it.

6. If you can stretch to it, buy a modem. On-line services and 'plug and play' easy-to-use communications software (no more lengthy configuration sessions) is set to explode.

7. If you want a Teletext downloading capability and don't want to install a circuit card yourself later, get one fitted when you buy your machine. WinTV is the most popular at the time of writing and we at Updata work very closely with this manufacturer.

8. Make sure the machine you buy comes with a minimum of one year's on-site warranty. If it comes with this kind of guarantee then you almost certainly will not have any serious problems.

9. Buy a brand of PC which is made by a large and reputable manufacturer. Normally they will have won a number of awards from the PC press.

10. View your PC purchase as a bit like buying a car. How long can you reasonably expect to use it for before upgrading to the next model?

CHAPTER THREE

Getting Data

• •

There are a number of ways to get data into your PC. The main types are as follows:

1. Manual Entry

2. Disk and CD–ROM

3. TV and Satellite Broadcast

4. Modem - On-line services

Manual Entry

You can type share prices manually into your PC. Beware that you will get lazy and tired of doing it, and in the end you will give up and lose track. Believe me, this happens even if you choose to type in ten shares once a week. This time is much better spent following your investments and spotting new opportunities, which are always available.

If you do choose this route (don't say I didn't warn you) then your most likely source of price information will be the share pages in the national newspapers. The broadsheets are best, with *The Financial Times* having the most in-depth coverage. However share prices are covered in nearly all papers including the tabloids. Many people prefer this cut down format of prices as finding all the ones you want can take hours in itself.

Disk and CD-ROM

Disk services have come and gone. There are two main problems; one is that the information is out of date as soon as it is copied, the other is that floppy disks don't have much capacity (1.44 MB). CD-ROM will present great opportunities for investors as the storage capacity is 650 MB. Many PCs don't have CD drives but most new ones do, so this medium is set to grow.

TV and Satellite Broadcast

There is more terrestrial and satellite broadcast information than most people know about. The increase of foreign channels on cable and satellite services is bringing the days of the global private investor much closer. The range of services, currently available are given below.

Teletext Broadcasts

This service was pioneered in Britain and spread east into continental Europe and parts of Asia, though it is not a standard in North America. Philips, the Dutch electronics group, have been instrumental in pushing this technology forward. There are likely to be some big changes with the convergence of TV and PC technologies. TV/Teletext cards are rapidly becoming a standard item in many PCs.

Teletext is a text service which is transmitted in the vertical blanking interval (vbi) with each television picture. These are leftover lines at the edges of pictures where data and other picture information can be sent. Teletext services were originally conceived as public broadcast services for education, hard of hearing and basic news services. The scope has increased such that most providers are now fully fledged screen based newspapers offering everything from up-to-the-minute news, sport, travel, entertainment listings, advertising and financial information.

Most European services offer price information on selected shares with some stock exchanges being more prepared to provide information than others. In Britain we are starting to see the kind of deregulation that has occurred in the US. This is essential if private investors are to compete on an even playing field with the professionals. In September 1994, Updata Software and Teletext (on ITV and Channel 4) offered a new service whereby all UK stocks became available on Channel 4. Although it is the previous day's closing prices transmitted from midnight, it is the ideal way to get price information onto your PC. We hope the next step is to improve the service to show end of day prices.

Teletext and the PC

One fact that many people don't appreciate is that whether you have a Teletext TV or not, Teletext data is still in the TV signal. To emphasise this fact during demonstrations, I often pull the aerial lead out of the socket to explain that all the prices are coming down this wire along with the TV picture. This means that with a PC Teletext decoder card you can turn your PC into a Teletext screen and collect and store the data. This process happens as follows:

So what interest does a software company have in working with Teletext to provide all UK share prices to a viewing audience of 1.5 million people each week? This is where the technology comes in. Over a number of years companies have sprung up that produce Teletext cards for the PC; this gives the user the ability to view Teletext pages on a PC screen in the same way as on television. This is only half the story because virtually anything is possible in software. Updata started out on the basis, if you can get it on a PC screen, you can get it into software. So the concept is very simple; with a Teletext circuit card and the right software you have a data gathering facility all for an amazing one-off cost which is a fraction of the annual cost not so long ago. Again that is not the full story. Now you have all the historical data stored on your PC, you can use other software for graphing, sophisticated technical analysis and portfolio management.

Real Time Data Feeds

This has been the staple diet of large City firms for years, but this is also beginning to change. There is now a range of services in the UK delivered over data broadcast on terrestrial TV and satellite.

At Updata this has become the next great bastion. Before our joint venture with Teletext the most common complaint with Teletext was that it did not cover all UK stocks. Now the biggest problem private investors have with price information is that they would like it to be real time and affordable.

There are a number of real time services for UK equity prices now available and we are already seeing some competition on price. A number of large media companies have announced they have plans to move into this area. There are even some PC manufacturers looking to target private investors with a range of on-line services.

Market-Eye in the UK, previously run by the London Stock Exchange, offers real time prices via a standard TV aerial. This service costs around £1,000 pa. plus exchange fees. The service is delivered over BBC1 datacast. This data cannot be viewed like Teletext. You need a PC Market-Eye card which goes inside the PC and you plug in a TV aerial. The concept is similar to Teletext downloading, but the data is real time. At Updata we have been working around this format for a couple of years and have recently introduced our flagship products for real time data storage and real time graphing. As PCs become more and more powerful, we are able to do more and more in software. There are also a number of exciting developments on the Internet, with some companies already starting to offer some real time prices.

The coming years will see some exciting developments for the screen based private investor. Those who do not get on board will be at a severe disadvantage in keeping on top of their investments.

Modem – On-line services

A modem is a device which enables you to receive data over standard telephone lines and download it into your computer. This is a more common method for collecting financial data in the US, where local calls are for a one-off cost. Certainly the next big explosion in the computer industry will be enhanced connectivity via a modem or a similar device. Teleworking (where people work from home) will drive this technology forward. Updata programmers work from home and check their work in by modem. I can log onto our network of PCs at Updata from anywhere in the world. Here, I can read, send or receive my electronic mail and data, or transfer documents and files from any member(s) of Updata staff.

The combination of personal computers and the international telephone networks forms the subject of our next chapter.

CHAPTER FOUR

The Internet – The Information Superhighway

No book that touches on personal computing would be complete without mentioning the Internet. This has seen such explosive growth, that I have decided to commit a full chapter to it. Born out of the US defence establishment, 'the net' as it is commonly known has seen a phenomenal number of people log on in the last couple of years. From a few hundred thousand to tens of millions of users worldwide in seemingly no time, this medium is demonstrative of the human races' hunger for information. Some pundits predict that the Internet is an experimental step towards something bigger. The Information Superhighway has suffered from some heavy roadwork's due to the rapidly increasing volume of traffic. It is, however, highly likely that the Internet will present great opportunities for the private investor.

What is it?

It is the best example of the Information Superhighway we have. Asking what the Internet is, is a bit like asking what road transport is. It is more of a subject or concept than a physical network. This makes it difficult to answer the regularly asked question and explains why many large organisations have been slow to identify its potential.

The network itself is best viewed as a net or a spiders web, with each of the threads representing the paths along which information can travel. Computer technology has meant that text, audio, pictures and even video information can be digitised into binary format. From here it can be compressed into a series of data packets, sent down the telephone line and reconstructed at the receiving end.

Where the net really comes into its own is the way in which this information can be transferred internationally for the cost of a local telephone call. There are a growing number of Internet providers who you can sign up with for a regular small monthly fee. Internet users around the world choose their nearest one so as to incur only local call charges while on-line. These providers effectively communicate with one another on a least cost route basis. Many of them have dedicated lines for sending vast amounts of information across oceans.

Each data packet carries the recipient's unique address and is effectively a small drop in the huge river of information flowing across the major routes.

The main functions of the Internet as an on-line user are covered in the remainder of this chapter.

Electronic Mail

This facility allows you to send and receive messages to and from anyone else (or group of interested parties) who also log onto the Internet. Electronic mail, e-mail for short, is like having your own text based answerphone on your PC. E-mail addresses have a standard layout as follows:

user@site.provider.business type.country

Where the user is the addressee, the site is the title or company providing a location, the provider is the Internet service provider (your connection to the net, such as Demon in the UK), business type is the type of institution (ie. co = company (.com for commercial in the US), ac – academic address in the UK (.edu in the US) and the country. A service provider is a company that you pay a low monthly fee to. They in turn act as your gateway to the Internet. Your personal e-mail address will have their name as part of it. This way the sender sends it to your service provider for when you next log on. This is explained further at the end of this chapter.

Hence,

Readers@updata.co.uk

E-mail is only a text based system and you have the ability to encrypt your messages, such that only the recipient can read it. Most Internet interfacing software support e-mail.

Usenet takes the concept a bit further to that of news groups and forums where large numbers of people can effectively communicate across the net. Most service providers, who you pay a small monthly fee to give you access to their news server. Most of the news will be from the core Internet user base from the US. Usenet is where the 'techie' element of the Internet tends to reside. Most new users of the net will find they access through the World Wide Web (WWW), covered below.

File Transfer Protocol

FTP is the standard use for downloading files on the net, though increasingly again this is automatically handled via links from WWW browsers. FTP accesses are logged at the point of download so the data provider can see who has been there.

World Wide Web

Brainchild of some scientists at the high energy particle physics laboratory at CERN in Switzerland, WWW started as a convenient way to store and retrieve documents and files. This is really what has made the net useable to a larger audience in the last few years.

The system is based on a series of links, such as hypertext, where one highlighted word will lead you to a topic. To get a feel of how hypertext works, go into a help file in any Windows compatible software program. You will see a series of highlighted words (normally in green). As you move the mouse cursor over these words the pointer changes to a hand implying you can uncover more in-depth information, relating to that word. Click and you will see more.

This concept could be employed with this book on an interactive CD-ROM for example. Instead of reading the whole of this book from start to finish, you could click on the words of interest as you see them and read the topics that appeal most to you.

If you want to witness the power of this technique, have a look at

. This and other titles was
of sales in hard copy
ercede these CD-ROMS as

worry because there is an
er and easier to use. By the
et could, and should, be as

)5 operating system has the
also providing their own
itrust investigation against
way as a PC user, sooner or

nternet

on locations, popping up in
me will happen in the UK.
ide Web site.
a.co.uk contain product
ns and answers. This opens
vnload all UK price histories
t need to be in the Teletext
ot requiring a Teletext card

There are other ventures emerging over the Internet. ESI, a UK based company, has announced its intention to post real time prices on the net. Initially, the LSE blocked this move, indicating that prices could be posted only after midnight. New EC directives mean that the exchange will find it increasingly difficult to prevent the spread of share prices. The days of real time prices at a very low cost cannot be far away.

Some other recent developments in the UK have been LIFFE posting futures data on the net and companies such as Tesco posting their company results on it as well. There should be an increasing amount of this which will enable investors to download them to be stored on their own PC.

You can get information directories on the net and you do get better at searching for what you want. For those who are more comfortable being paper based than screen based you can buy monthly magazines on the Internet which list the latest sites to visit. This sounds more like a brochure for tourists, I know, but this language reflects how interactive the net is becoming.

Closed User Groups and On-Line Services

There are some sites, or areas of sites, on the net which you have to pay to access. There are also others such as CompuServe (3m users worldwide) which offer a range of pay as you go services. These services are often gateways to access larger databases. Other companies offer electronic Bulletin Board Systems (BBS) for customers to get information via a direct link.

These kinds of on-line services are becoming cheaper all the time. Information that is effectively in the public domain for the private investor is heading towards zero cost. This will take us to the level playing field that is well overdue.

How to get on-line

The first step is to get a modem from a computer supplier. Modems will be quoted with different speeds, known as baud rate. The faster ones will be more expensive, but a worthwhile investment as you will spend less time on-line, downloading information. I have a 14,400 Bd modem which plugs into my portable PC and I wish I had a 28,800 one. You can get an internal card, or an external one if you don't want to open up your PC.

Once you are hooked up, plug the telephone lead into a phone socket. You can get a double adaptor for a couple of pounds so your phone can stay plugged in. Modems can be difficult to set up, although Windows 95 'plug and play' technology is making it easier. Have a go first time, but be prepared to get someone to do it for you if you are not technically minded.

To get on the Internet, buy an Internet magazine and look up your nearest service provider so you only pay local call rate to be on-line. A service provider called Demon is the most popular in the UK. The same magazine should give you a guide of interesting 'sites' to visit. You will go through some trials and tribulations, but on the whole it becomes very worthwhile and things are set to get better as it becomes a more common part of all our lives.

Appendix One at the end of this book covers a number of site addresses where you can get financial information. New sites are becoming available all the time as well.

CHAPTER FIVE

Software

• •

There are several packages available in the UK for the private investor. There is a brief summary in this chapter under the following categories:

Operating Systems

Word Processors, Spreadsheets and Databases

Price Display Software

Charting or Graphing Packages

Portfolio Management and Personal Finance

Operating Systems

Before we look at the various packages available, we should mention the main operating systems available. Software falls under two categories,

DOS based and Windows based. MS-DOS (Disk Operating System) was launched by Microsoft over a decade ago. This is the command based language that allows software programs to utilise the computer.

The computer industry says that "DOS is DEAD" due to the phenomenal success of Microsoft Windows. There are still many DOS programs around and a number of investment software packages which may suit the needs of some private investors.

Windows

Microsoft have really driven the PC revolution to the non technical user with their Windows Graphical User Interface (GUI). The key advantages of Windows are:

1. You can run more than one program at a time.

2. You can move data easily between programs.

3. You can see a number of things at once.

4. Look and feel are the same generally in different programs.

5. It is a very intuitive environment.

DOS and Windows are normally pre-supplied on most new PCs. 1995 has seen the most significant product launch the PC industry has known. Windows '95 from Microsoft is the next generation of 32 Bit operating system. Sometimes called Windows 4, it really is the second generation of Windows as it is so dramatically different from the first versions.

The key benefits of this new environment are as Windows plus:

1. The interface is much easier and intuitive to use, especially for new users to the system.

2. 'Plug and Play' technology means your system copes better with new devices, such as modems and printers.

3. It is faster, providing greater productivity.

4. Multitasking means while you wait in one program, you can do things in others.

Also central to Microsoft's view of the future is Object Linking and Embedding (OLE). This standard was very sluggish and impractical in the old 16 Bit Windows environment. Now under 32 Bits it is great. What does it mean for you the user? An example is all the embedded graphs in this book. Unfortunately they are not embedded as objects. If they were, every time I opened the document in my word processor they would update themselves. They could be live in the document as I view it. This doesn't sound that useful, but brokers will not be the only ones wanting to produce their own tailor made market reports each morning. You will have the power for your PC to do this unattended, print it out for yourself and read it at breakfast every day. Many Updata users have their PCs come on automatically on a time clock each day and collect their data from them. They can go away on holiday for weeks while their PC gathers data on their behalf.

Should you move to Windows '95

At the time of writing the reaction to Microsoft's new operating system has been very mixed. The main complaint that is filtering through is that the system requirements are greater than those that Windows 3.1 required. There was in fact a very similar problem when people moved from DOS to Windows a few years ago. While everyone has the daggers out for Microsoft, it is likely that the fuss will pass and computer technology will more than grow into the new environment.

If you are about to purchase a system, I would recommend that you go for a specification that is adequate for Windows '95. The main reason for this is that you will benefit from many of the exciting changes that occur over the coming years and the specific benefits listed previously.

Word Processors, Spreadsheets and Databases

These are the big three in mainstream applications and three US corporations dominate, Microsoft, Novel (the networking giant) and Lotus (now owned by IBM).

The market leader in word processing software used to be Word Perfect, now owned by Novel. However, Microsoft have gained dominance with their Word for Windows package.

Word processing is probably the single most useful task for anyone who has a PC in their home or office. Writing letters, creating documents and having essential tools such as a spell checker are a must. Most of the mainstream products come packed with functionality. At a recent Parliamentary Information Technology Committee meeting, Dr Peter Cochrane (BTs No.3), asked how many people were more creative than they had ever been using their PC. The response was unanimous. A single user armed with a PC can now do what a large company with a typing pool did ten or fifteen years ago.

The spreadsheet was invented by a company called Visicalc soon after the PC was born. Lotus soon took over to dominate with its 123 software. Once more Microsoft has stolen the lead more recently with its product Excel.

For those who haven't used one, the spreadsheet is the best thing since sliced bread. You can now produce financial projections and accounts in minutes and tailor this powerful tool to your needs every time you use it. The principle is one of a series of cells. Each cell can contain a formula that takes values from other cells to create the answers you need. I believe that Microsoft Excel is the best software package ever written. It is the kind of product we at Updata aspire to.

Below is an example of an Excel spreadsheet which we supply with every Updata package. It is very basic, but the description below explains how it works.

A	B	C	D	E	F	G	H	I	J	K	L	M
Title	Price	Qnty	Value	BuyAt	Value	BuyOn	SoldAt	SoldOn	Chg	Prof	%Prof	%ARR
SHARES												
Abbey Nt	532	200	1064	426	852	18-Dec-94			106	212	25	30
Asda	104	1000	1040	55	550	18-Feb-94			49	490	89	54
BP	468.5	500	2343	229	1145	26-Nov-92			240	1198	105	36
Br Steel	182.5	500	913	74	370	04-Feb-93			109	543	147	55
M & S	433	400	1732	254	1016	10-Jul-91			179	716	70	17
NatWest	630	300	1890	480	1440	28-Aug-94			150	450	31	28
Total			8981		5373			Averages	139	601	78	37

A. Name of share, typed in.

B. Price - live linked from Updata Teleshares (Dynamic Data Exchange - DDE).

C. Quantity, entered manually.

D. Value in pounds, Formula cells B x C.

E. Price bought at - entered manually.

F. Value when bought - C x E.

G. Date bought - entered manually.

H. Sold At - entered manually.

I. Sold On - entered manually.

J. Change, Formula cells H - E if sold or B - E if not.

K. Profit in pounds, C x J.

L. Return %, Formula H/B (or E) x 100.

M. Annualised Return, Formula L x 365/(I - G), if not sold (Today - G).

Data Feed Integration

For many PC users this is not a software issue, as it is not seen. In real terms software falls into two categories – underlying computer code, low level and interface or front end, high level. This chapter mainly covers the latter, as this is what the user sees. Data feed integration is low level code and this is where the serious programming challenges lie. While this is unseen by the user, properly designed frameworks and structures are an essential foundation to smooth data collection for your investment software. At Updata we have been working on the next generation framework for data collection for over a year and half and we will be launching products based on this new technology in the coming months and years.

Central to this framework is the ability for the user to plug in data sources of their choice. This means that you may choose to run on a free data source such as Teletext as well as real time feeds of your choice. We believe this will become an increasingly powerful proposition for the investor. Choose your software and plug in the data sources of your choice. In the end you only have one interface to learn and use. Even corporate customers are coming to see the benefits of members of staff having to learn one interface for different information sources.

Price Display Software

City screens were traditionally monitors displaying prices from a dedicated data feed. The bulk of the processing was done on mainframe systems at the information provider. As PC technology improved and the Windows environment infiltrated the dealing room a new type of software emerged. Windows offered the key advantage that people could have multiple screens, or windows, all on one screen, or in one window.

Nearly all information, or data feed, providers offer price display software as part of their package. Because they are not focused purely on software, there is an increasing tendency for software houses to work to provide better software than the feed providers. UK companies such as Reuters and ICV have started to deploy an open systems strategy, because they are starting to recognise that customers want the choice of increased flexibility. In short, the information systems market is fragmenting in the 1990s, much the same way as the computer industry did in the 1980s.

There are a few price display software systems available in the corporate market. These are high level systems which are out of the price range of private investors, as are the feeds they run on.

At Updata, we have tried to emulate trends in the corporate market and find ways of bringing them to private investors cost effectively. On the whole there are no dedicated price display packages available other than the ones Updata provides. We started this process with the introduction of Teleshares in association with Teletext last year. Teleshares is now set to become available in the high street at a price starting point of around £50. Another product, born of our new technology is Trader, an advanced price display and storage package. A screen of this is shown on the next page.

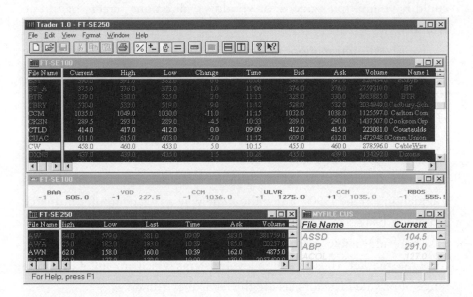

Source: Updata

Charting or Graphing Packages

Charting packages were really the beginning of computerised analysis for the private investor. Certainly during the 1980s Synergy, a UK based company, were the market leaders in DOS based technical analysis software. Synergy have stayed with DOS and have consequently perhaps missed some opportunities offered by Windows. The other main companies in the UK market are Fairshares, Indexia, Meridian and Updata. The two biggest players in the US, Supercharts, from Omega and Metastock, from Equis have also managed to penetrate the UK. This has been to a smaller extent due to lack of tailoring to UK investors, data sources and no UK based technical support. There is also a growing band of small home based outfits launching software products that are mainly DOS based.

Purchasing charting software with this backdrop of choice does not make the process any easier for the UK investor. As with PCs, a simple checklist of questions follows:

1. Has the company managed to keep up with the technology and what are its plans for the future?

2. What is the policy for upgrades, once you are on board?

3. Is there somewhere you can see it, trade shows, open days, shops, demo suites, demo disks or trial packages?

4. Are there any hidden extras, like data or support fees?

5. What is the policy on technical support?

6. What is the compatibility with other software packages?

7. Are there any press reviews available, third party endorsements, user testimonies etc.?

8. Is there a user group, forum, newsletter, or place where users can meet?

9. What is the product documentation like, are there any on screen tutorials to help you get to grips with it?

10. Does the company have any stockbroker relationships?

This is not the place for me to review software products, suffice to say Updata provides a range of products. All the graphs in this book have been cut from Updata software and pasted into the word processor used. Reviews and surveys are starting to appear more frequently in the various investment magazines and PC press.

Portfolio Management and Personal Finance

Personal Finance Software showed how important a category of software it has become when Microsoft attempted to take over Intuit last year. Intuit had become the market leader with its flagship product, Quicken and had established itself firmly in the electronic home banking arena, where Microsoft itself was keen to be. The takeover never went through because of Microsoft's difficulties in a number of areas with the Federal Trade Commission. This has left Intuit as the major player and Microsoft competing aggressively with its Money product.

Intuit have been very effective at producing and marketing their software as easy to use software that organises your finances painlessly. They have also showed themselves to be more committed to the UK market than most other US software houses in that they have tailored the UK versions to the market in this country. Apart from being a very effective tool for keeping on top of your bank account, loans and finances generally, Quicken has some features built in for the UK investor.

While Quicken is not a dedicated portfolio management package, it does come with some basic facilities which become quite powerful when linked through to data that is exported from packages such as Teleshares. Quicken does not deal with Capital Gains Tax calculations, but Quick Tax, also from Intuit, does. Each of these products retails for less than £50, and provides excellent value for money.

On the whole I haven't covered portfolio management in this book as I believe most UK investors appear to be obsessed with counting their money and worrying about their tax liability. I will look at what makes a successful investor rather than an effective generator of reports. Investors must focus more on buying and especially on selling, the more common problem. This is covered more under Chapter Ten *Monitoring* in the next section. As I said in the Introduction, tax considerations should not be the main factor in making buy and sell decisions. Shares must be bought and sold on **their** merits, not yours.

PART TWO

Using Your System

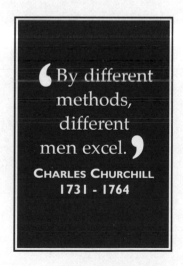

'By different methods, different men excel.'

CHARLES CHURCHILL
1731 - 1764

CHAPTER SIX

Basic Technical Analysis

● ●

Over the years, I have met many investors who have succeeded by using different strategies. The common element was they all had a methodical approach and were not emotional about their decisions. They are prepared to accept they got it wrong and cut their losses, where appropriate. If you don't already have an approach that works, or want a better one, simple technical analysis will probably be central to your strategy of using a computer for investing.

So you have got your computer, information source and software system in place and are now committed to adopting a more methodical approach. One of your first steps is to get a basic understanding of technical analysis.

Some basic principles

This chapter serves as background information and reference to the 'art' of 'technical analysis' often referred to as charting.

Charts, or graphs, have two main functions:

1. Presentation of historical performance and the latest price changes at a glance.
2. The ability to analyse this information in order to make investment decisions.

It is recognised that some investors may use graphs for the first function only. They may be deterred from the second function by the apparent complexity that even the term 'technical analysis' implies, or feel that learning to use it would be too time consuming. I always say to investors that seeing the graph is most of it, establishing a trend is most of the rest and tools used thereafter are mainly for confirmation. It should be made clear that charting can, and indeed often should, be kept as simple as possible.

Where to find them

Charts have become an everyday, in fact every second, part of financial markets. They are on the screens in nearly all the market dealing rooms around the world. In most major international trading centres charts reach the man on the street in the daily newspapers. It is interesting to note that many small or private investors in these places, especially in Asia, have managed to keep up with financial markets better than in Britain. Unfortunately, we have to look harder to find charts. They appear in financial magazines, City circulars, and occasionally in the City pages of newspapers.

Investment software packages allow private investors and companies to have a system which is comparable to the incredibly sophisticated equipment that the City uses. You no longer need to rely so heavily on your bank, your broker, or your financial adviser for information. You now have the information and the ability to analyse it so that you can make your own decisions.

What charts represent

A common view is that charts indicate the balance, or imbalance, between buyers and sellers in a market and from this one can deduce when the market is 'overbought' or 'oversold'. This is not a bad interpretation, but it is a long way from actually understanding what charts represent and why they work.

Many people, professionals among them, use charts without understanding why they work and still manage to profit from them by just knowing the buy and sell signals that they give. However, better understanding must lead to fewer misinterpretations and less doubt when making decisions.

Charts have two immediate advantages. Firstly, they present a picture of the historic price movement and the mind is able to assimilate this information more quickly than a list of tabulated figures. Secondly, any major price change will be noticed immediately.

A good understanding of market behaviour can come from an analogy with the tidal motion of the sea.

Say the tide is going out quite fast when it begins to slow down, mainly due to a decreasing mass of water behind it and an increasing mass providing resistance ahead of it. It gradually slows to a point where the water is 'slack' (low tide) and then the tide begins to come in moving slowly at first gathering speed then slowing to a 'slack' state again (high tide) and then turning the other way going out again (ie. full cycle).

Investors behave in a remarkably similar manner. 'Running for the door' is an expression often used when many people are trying to get out of a particular market. The 'tide' begins to turn and more and more people sell until buyers start returning to the market turning the 'tide' back the other way, where 'panic buying' starts to occur for fear of missing the boat. Unfortunately, financial markets are more complicated, with many cycles of different length and magnitude. However, in a similar manner to tides, markets do follow natural phenomenon. This is because they directly represent crowd behaviour.

My view is that the graph represents everything that everyone in the market already knows about the stock. If it is not in the graph, you have a very remote chance of knowing it anyway. Over 80% of UK equities are owned by institutions who spend enormous sums researching the companies in which they invest. Private investors may be better studying the effect rather than identifying the cause. It is our obsession with diagnosis that often wastes our time. Patients like to know what is wrong with them more than what will make them better. Do we need to know the reasons why a stock is under or over-valued?

Why charts work

Crowd behaviour, and therefore markets, can be predicted; while an individual's behaviour tends to be unpredictable. As markets mimic natural cycles, mathematical principles may be used to analyse them. It can be considered that each price movement is mathematically related to the preceding price movements.

As with the tide, reversals in price occur at extremes. If an extreme level is breached then it is human nature to react to this. A precedent is set for movement in what might be termed as new ground. The extreme levels in charts are known as support and resistance.

A trading range is normally within a trend which is sloping. The general direction of the trend will therefore be up or down. Otherwise the trend will be horizontal, often called 'trading sideways'.

Sceptics will say 'Ah yes, but the whole thing is unpredictable, what if bad economic figures come out and the market falls? How can charts foresee that?' It is true that charts cannot foresee bad economic statistics. However, they can tell the level of market vulnerability or resilience and the reaction can be analysed to indicate the most likely new direction. It will be shown that charts cut down the element of risk and uncertainty, which often lead to unnecessary panic decisions.

Finally, the biggest enemy of the investor is doubt. It is possible that a signal may be contrary to the popular opinion prevailing, and crowd pressure to ignore a signal may be extremely strong. Charts reduce susceptibility to crowd pressure. This doubt produces fear which closes the mind to rational thought. Fearful investors will deal blindly. Indeed, investing without charts, especially once one has become used to them, makes one feel as if one is blindfolded. We are regularly indecisive. The graph dramatically reduces this by providing information in a form which eliminates guesswork and allows one, in a rational and decisive manner, to picture what is most likely to happen.

Basic principles

This section explains the ideas behind charting and how various indicators are derived. The basic concepts are looked at under the headings of *Trends, Cycles, Overlays, Averages,* and *Periods.* This leads on to *Targets, Price Levels* and *Stop-Losses.* Utilising these ideas in practice is covered in the following chapters.

Trends

We have established that charts can follow trends. Prices oscillate about a 'central trendline'. A better way of looking at trends, however, is to draw trendlines across the turning (reversal) points of the cycles as shown on the opposite page. These lines of 'support' and 'resistance' are not always parallel as in this case. The area between them is known as the 'trend channel' or 'band'.

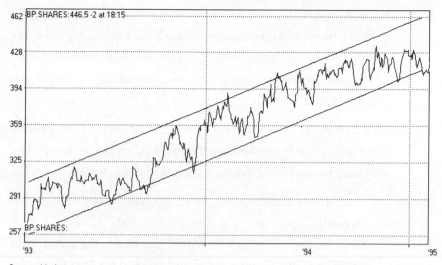

Source: Updata

BP with an auto-trend channel showing general trend.

The advantage of this is immediately apparent. One can see where to expect a price reversal and how far it is to the other extreme trendline. Also, when the trendline is broken a signal is given that the price line has entered into new ground often called 'new territory'. This is known as a 'breakout' and possible variations are discussed in the next chapter. Sometimes only a clear resistance line can be found while support is not clearly apparent and vice versa.

A common situation in financial markets is where the price line follows:

1. A primary, or major, trend usually lasting for more than a year and may last several years. It is this trend that normally defines a 'bull' (rising) or a 'bear' (falling) market.

2. Secondary, or intermediate, trends are normally reversals to the primary trend and may last anywhere from a few weeks to a few months. They usually retrace between one third and two thirds of the gain or loss registered by the preceding swing in the primary trend

3. Day-to-day, or minor, trends are fluctuations which usually have little bearing on the longer term trends. They normally last less than several days but may last up to a few weeks.

Occasionally trendlines may curve slightly. This has the implication that the trend is speeding up or slowing down. This leads us to the notion that while the price line is oscillating within the trend, the trend itself can be oscillating in a much longer trend and so on. This idea forms the basis of the concept of cycles.

Cycles

As with trends, the validity of a cycle is governed by how closely and for how long the cycle has been followed. The cycle is basically the price line and, like trends, there may be cycles within cycles or cycles of different lengths. These cycles could well be occurring within different level trends. If we consider the analogy we made with the behaviour of the tides, the three levels of cycle can be likened to the ocean's tide, waves and ripples.

In order to identify cycles it is necessary to look a long way back into price histories. It will be much harder to spot clear cycles in some price lines than in others. There are some methods, such as measuring the distance between successive peaks or just seeing which moving averages work best.

Another way of avoiding being distracted by the short-term fluctuations within minor trends is to use averages, discussed shortly. A cycle is primarily identified by what is known as its 'period'. This is simply the time that it takes for a complete cycle to occur. Identifying the period is essential to carrying out technical analysis using the methods which follow.

Overlays

A very simple and clearly useful concept in charting is the use of overlays. This facility allows one to see the performance of one investment in comparison to another.

The advantage of using overlays is that they allow comparative analysis. For example over two price histories both investments may well have followed each other for a time and then diverged. For instance, they may be shares in the same industrial sector and one has either under or outperformed allowing the investor to spot a possible 're-rating' of one back in line with the other.

A re-rating of one of the stocks should occur if the divergence had no apparent reason behind it, and further analysis would reveal which one is likely to move. A divergence can be further reinforced when comparing more than two stocks from the same sector clearly showing the odd one out, ie. 3 stocks are more conclusive than 2. This leads us to another common example of comparing a share relative to an index.

Apart from spotting divergence one can also pinpoint similarities; eg. whether one investment is sensitive or influenced by another. The old saying 'when Wall Street sneezes, London catches a cold' can be verified by overlaying the Dow Jones and FT-SE 100 (Footsie) indices. One can see how underlying commodities such as gold, oil or even currencies affect shares of companies that trade in them.

Averages

The concept of averages, often called moving averages in charting, forms the basis of some of the more powerful higher order, short-term, technical analysis indicators. Unfortunately, as a result, many investors overlook them when in fact they serve an important function in chart analysis.

A moving average smoothes the erratic short-term fluctuations of the price line. Each value on the average line is calculated by taking the latest price and adding a chosen number of previous days' prices and dividing by the number chosen. The following day the process is the same but the price of the chosen number of days ago is dropped due to the addition of the latest price; hence the name 'moving' average.

There are two ways of using averages in charting. They can be used in conjunction with the price line, or with another average of a different averaging period. The longer the averaging period chosen the less sensitive the average is to a dramatic price change, and the further it will be from the price line. The shorter the averaging period, the closer the average to the price line. Indeed, a one day moving average is the same as a price line of daily prices.

The concept of averages allows one to assess a particular price change in the context of the recent behaviour of the price line. The fact that it is moving means that the standard of the price line is constantly being revised.

Periods

Before we go any further, the idea of using cycle periods must be addressed. The period of a cycle is the time it takes for one complete cycle to occur. In other words the time that has elapsed from one point to another where the cycle begins to repeat or retrace itself. The diagram below shows a very simple example of this. Three complete cycles about a central axis are drawn, with a half and a quarter cycle clearly marked. Looking at this cycle period more closely we can see that if we take any point along the curve and draw a horizontal line back a full period length we cover every position of the three cycles within the period.

This is an example of a very simple cycle and the price line is normally much more complex. The graph on page 70 shows a real case

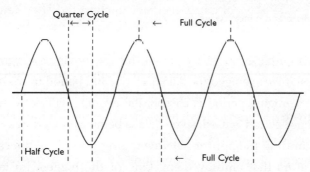

of cyclical behaviour in financial markets. There are two cycles marked; an intermediate and a minor cycle. Although this example is more complex, the principles are much the same. The central axis is no longer horizontal, but instead it has a gradient in the trend direction. The cycle is still oscillating about this axis, except it is not as symmetrical.

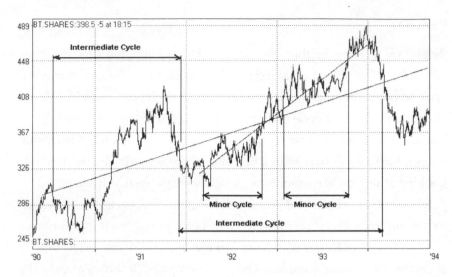

Source: Updata

BT – intermediate and minor cycles.

From this simple example, we can see that the moving averaging period would be best if we averaged the data back one full period from each point. If a shorter averaging period is chosen, the average will not catch all the data. If a longer period is used, some data is being averaged twice.

Understanding the appropriate averaging periods is the essence of using indicators that employ them. One of the biggest mistakes that many people make when using technical analysis is choosing averaging periods that bear no relationship to the price line of the share that they are trying to chart. Some analysts may swear by a specific averaging period and use it on everything that they chart. This can only be a hit or miss technique. It is hard to understand why they believe that this will work for a range of shares with such a huge variation in behavioural patterns. Period optimisation using cycles, tailors analysis to each individual charting exercise.

Financial markets often follow natural cycles as they are based on crowd behaviour. Mathematical sequences such as Fibonacci numbers are often surprisingly accurate if you don't know where to start in choosing your averaging period. The sequence is based on the twelfth century mathematician's studies of natural phenomena and these principles were introduced to financial markets by the renowned Wall Street trader W.D. Gann. The sequence is derived by adding the two previous numbers to arrive at the next, to give: 1 2 3 5 8 13 21 34 55 89 144... and so on. Using these numbers as averaging periods is a quick route to taking a view over the chosen period.

These numbers are very often approximately equal to the cycle period length. Therefore, when estimating the period length it is worth bearing them in mind.

Higher Order Charting Indicators

This area of technical analysis is closely linked to what has just been discussed. A good way of understanding why higher order indicators work is to make an analogy with distance, speed, and acceleration of a motor car.

For example:

A man in his car accelerates and immediately he feels himself being thrust back in his seat. Distance and speed are increasing dramatically but already the driver notices that he is having difficulty maintaining the thrust. Therefore, acceleration is decreasing and soon he notices that the speedometer is climbing much more slowly at high speed. He has his foot flat to the floor and he has reached a point where the car will not go any faster. So he eases his foot on the accelerator, and acceleration is now acting in the other direction mainly due to friction on the road and air resistance. Therefore, he is slowing down. Then the brakes are applied with deceleration now increased, speed decreasing more dramatically, but with distance increasing until the car stops.

The essence of this analogy is that higher order indicators (similar in nature to speed or acceleration) can detect movements in the price line (synonymous with distance) before they actually occur. It is this major principle that allows technical indicators to help sense price reversals in financial markets before they actually occur.

These indicators are covered later. Many investors become too focused on these tools at the expense of first principles. The help is in anticipating signals or reversals. This should be used to be aware that a change may be about to happen. There are many false alarms. Unfortunately some investors trade on the anticipation. You should always wait for a conclusive signal such as a trend being clearly breached or a significant reversal in price.

Targets, price levels and stop-losses

Buying

The concept of targets is one of studying levels of the price line. While it is accepted that the million dollar question is not usually what to do, but in fact when to do it, it is often important to know the extent of price movements. The dilemma of when to buy and when to sell is greatly reduced using the technical analysis indicators we have mentioned. There are, however, times where one might be happy, particularly with selling, to base decisions on the extent of a price movement. This can help to assess profitability. The projected movement for buying may not be enough to cover dealing costs, or may be lower than the return another investment might offer, or simply may be too small to warrant any action. An example may be a narrow trend channel, that is not upward and the move from the bottom to the top not great enough.

When a line of resistance is clearly breached it can become a new line of support for the new trading range. The reverse may also occur if the price line falls through a support line, that is, this now becomes a level of resistance.

The simplest way of assessing the likely extent of a price rise is to follow the line of resistance for an uptrend to the required date in the future and note the price level. Similarly one can follow a support line for a downtrend to assess the extent of a fall by a future date.

Selling

Another form of target is a 'stop-loss' line. This is a well known investment principle whereby the investor decides at which level after a price reversal he will 'buy' or 'sell'. This in effect places a criteria on the price line in order to consider a reversal valid.

The stop-loss technique is normally applied to a downturn in prices. The most successful traders in any market are the ones who keep their losses small. For example if a limit of a 5% fall in price is decided this means that an investment will be sold when that level is breached limiting the loss to 5%.

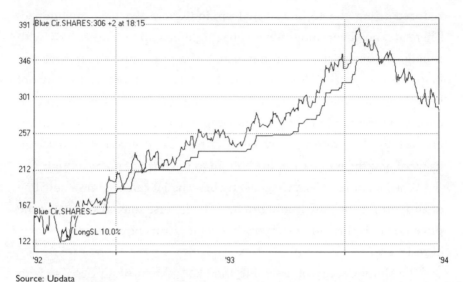

Source: Updata

The stop-loss only moves up when the share price exceeds the
previous peak. Otherwise it moves sideways.

This can be taken a step further by actually moving the limit with the
price line in order to protect profits. This means that the rise can be
followed until it falls back by the limit decided. Looking at the diagram
above we can see an example of this very simple principle being
employed. Most investors use a stop-loss of 5% or 10%, but ideally one
should study the price line history to arrive at the best level. The smaller
the percentage the more sensitive the stop-loss. It will give more signals
and more false alarms as well. Too big a percentage, however, and there
is a risk of missing valid signals altogether. It is a fairly crude technique
but can be useful especially when deciding whether to 'hold' or 'sell'.
One may be happy to take a profit.

Using stop-loss allows you to follow the four key rules to investing:

1. Cut losses

2. Cut losses

3. Cut losses

4. Let profits run

CHAPTER SEVEN

Using Technical Indicators

● ●

This chapter shows how each of the indicators may be used. While there is no particular order in which the indicators should be used, the progression followed here is the most logical. As one goes through the analysis process, one is gathering more and more knowledge about an investment as each indicator is utilised. If one particular indicator is giving a negative signal contrary to the others then some serious questions must be asked. It must be remembered that one indicator alone usually means very little. Indeed they are a set of tools that become very powerful when used in conjunction with one another. Trading strategies are discussed in the following chapters.

Trends

The first thing to establish is that the price line actually follows a trend. A central trendline, or rule of thumb, can be drawn over the price history as a whole. This will now make the general trend very obvious but it probably won't place enough emphasis on the current situation. In other words, the trendline needs to be drawn from the beginning of the present short-term trend.

An approximate trend channel can be drawn with support and resistance lines running parallel to the centre line. We can tell whether the trend is well followed by how often the peaks of the price line touch the resistance line and the troughs touch the support line. If the trend is well followed then it is very likely that it will continue to be. From this we can deduce that when the price line has fallen to the support line it will reverse direction and move upward to the resistance line. Similarly if the price line approaches the resistance line, we could expect a reversal at, or near (depending how close the reversal points have been to the trendlines over the price history), the line and the price line to subsequently fall to the support line.

Unfortunately charting is not always that simple. In most cases the support and resistance lines do not run parallel to each other and therefore have to be drawn manually. These will, however, usually run in a similar direction to the central trendline. A support line can easily be drawn so as to touch the troughs of the reversal points. A resistance line can be drawn in a similar manner across the peaks of the reversal points.

The drawing of trendlines will often lead to a triangle. If there is a triangle formation or the trend channel has been broken then we have what is known as a 'breakout'.

Source: Updata

Asda drift sideways out of the downward trend channel, and takes another two years to fully turn and breakout.

Breakouts

Eventually trendlines will be broken because of an unwillingness to continue following the current trend. Either because a price range is too cheap and there are more buyers than sellers, or because the price range is too expensive and there are more sellers than buyers.

Buy Signals

1. If a 'price line' penetrates upwards through the resistance level of a downward trend channel by a few percent or more, the trend can be considered to be broken indicating a price reversal. An upward trend channel should now start to form.

2. If the penetration is upward through an upward trend channel, this indicates that the price line is in new territory. The most likely scenarios are that either the trend channel will become dramatically steeper or the resistance line will become a new level of support.

Source: Updata

Royal Bank breaks into new territory and more than doubles in a year.

Sell Signals

1. If a 'price line' penetrates downwards through the support level of an upward trend channel by a few percent or more the trend can be considered to be broken signifying a price reversal. A downward trend channel should now start to form.

2. If the penetration is downward through a downward trend channel this indicates that the price line is in new territory and the support line is likely to become a new level of resistance.

Source: Updata

Forte: Sideways triangles can go either way, even in a bull market.

The more cautious investor may use a higher breakout percentage than 3%. Some chartists use 5%. However the best method is to try to spot how rigidly the price line has stayed within the trend channel over the price history. It is so often the case with charting that past performance gives a better indication than more general hard and fast rules.

It is often much better to draw longer lines that don't precisely intersect the price line. Although the licence is there for slight variations it must be remembered that the less rigidly the trend is adhered to, the more unpredictable the subsequent behaviour of the price line.

The concept of trends has been simplified here to represent the principles. Daily or hourly fluctuations make a price line look jagged. One begins to see more than one possible trendline and the picture becomes complicated. The essence of charting is visualisation and this comes with practice. It is more an art than a science. Generally the more times a 'price line' bounces off a trendline (ie. the more reversal points that the trendline passes through), the more valid the trend. Invariably a minimum of three points are required to verify a valid trend. The more points there are, the more likely the price line will bounce off it again. However, trend channels do not last forever due to breakouts so other indicators are necessary.

Overlays

There is a stockmarket adage; 'Never trade against the market.' This simply means that if the market is falling one should not expect, bar exceptional circumstances, to make a large profit on a particular share. Strong stocks, at best, will often stagnate in a falling market. The FT-SE 100 index is a good measure of the volume of trading in the London stockmarket as a whole. Therefore the adage may be read as 'don't trade against the Footsie'.

The graph on page 83 shows the FT-SE 100 rebased to start with the GEC price history and GEC relative to the index (The Relative). The rebased graph shows that GEC under-performed the FT-SE 100 index over the past twelve years. The relative graph adds an extra dimension, by showing the share's true performance against the market. For instance there are times when GEC is rising, but the relative is falling, indicating that the share is not rising as fast as the market. There are also points where the relative is rising, while the market is falling, showing GEC's resilience.

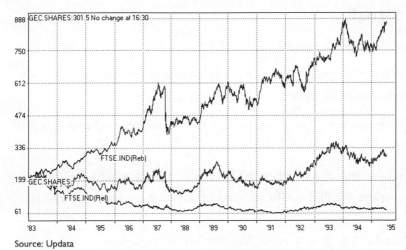

888 GEC.SHARES:301.5 No change at 16:30

Source: Updata

GEC's periods of under-performance are more clearly shown by the relative.

Averages

Following on from what was discussed in the previous chapter, we now need to be able to interpret the signals that we may be given by using the moving averages in the two different ways. Selecting the appropriate averaging period is discussed under **Periods** on page 85.

First, we shall consider the moving average against the price line. When the price line cuts down through the moving average this may be regarded as a sell signal and when it cuts up through the moving average this may be considered to be a buy signal. If the price line is moving within a narrow band the moving average may give many signals. One has to assess whether this band is wide enough to make trading profitable.

Buy Signals

There are three such signals:

1. When the price line moves up through its moving average which is itself rising.

2. When the price line moves down towards its moving average and then bounces off it.

3. When the share price temporarily falls through its moving average, which is still rising, and then bounces back through it.

Often the use of a moving average on its own gives a rather late signal and it is common practice to use a combination of moving averages, as we have already discussed. This not only gives better signals but has the added advantage of highlighting which averaging period works best. When both moving averages cross and point upwards in the same direction this is a strong buy indicator and is known as a 'golden cross'. When both moving averages draw towards each other and don't cross, this is usually a bearish indicator. It is essential that the cross actually occurs and should one of the averages be pointing downwards while the other points upwards this is not a golden cross.

A 'dead cross' is exactly the opposite of a golden cross, ie. when both moving averages point downwards. If the shorter average cuts down through the longer one this is a sell signal.

Sell Signals

1. When the price line is moving down through its moving average which is itself moving down.

2. When the price line moves up towards its moving average, then bounces off it.

3. When the price line temporarily rises through its moving average which itself is falling, then falls back through it.

This is a rather brief summary of the concept of moving averages. With experience one will find that one can look directly at the short-term indicators like OBOS and MACD to begin with (see Chapter Twelve *Getting more sophisticated*). One may only feel the need to look at moving averages to further clarify the picture. Again users should not go out of their way to remember each case and just use these pages as a reference.

Periods

Choosing the appropriate averaging period is the critical part of using averages, as well as oscillators. The longer the averaging period, the fewer, or the later, the number of signals that will be given, and hence the fewer profit opportunities. An averaging period of one cycle length is a good place to start. One should also check to see that the moving average has given the appropriate signals in the past, ie. that the price line has moved up after a buy signal. How substantial the moves have been is an indication of how well that averaging period is working. If too many small moves have been detected as signals then the averaging period is too short. The next step may be to choose a period which is of the next greatest length and go through the same process of studying how well it gives signals.

If, on the other hand, the average does not pick up substantial moves in the price line then a period of the next lowest length should be used. The need for this adjustment will most probably be due to the poor estimation of the cycle period in the first place (ie. being slightly out with the period length). It is basically a process of trial and error until the averages give good signals historically.

The other possibility is that the price line follows no cyclical pattern at all, which is not uncommon. Averages will do little for you in this case and you will probably need to rely on trends.

Volumes

The level of volume indicates people's willingness to deal. Data on levels of volume in financial markets is relatively limited.

A low level of volume shows that there is uncertainty about the future direction of the market, while a high level shows a high degree of confidence about the future direction of the market. A conflict in volume and movement in price reflects traders' attitudes towards the market. For example, it is a familiar story in markets that traders have marked stocks up sharply but there has been little turnover. It is hardly surprising that in this instance, prices invariably retreat to match the level of volume.

Chapter Twelve covers volume and liquidity by looking more closely at high/low spikes on graphs.

CHAPTER EIGHT

Practice makes perfect - Profit

There is no question that the longer you observe markets, the more you learn. One of our greatest challenges at Updata has been to find ways to help investors make money on the stockmarket. Thousands of people have asked 'can I really get a system that will work for me?' There are a number of ways you can practice playing the market:

1. You can run a 'ghost' portfolio by hand picking stocks you have researched. This gets pretty laborious as it can take a while to see results.

2. You can buy and sell shares in the market. Without practice and experience of watching markets, this can be expensive.

3. You can invest in a software package that allows you to look at a number of graphs back over time. We have been known to encourage people to cover half the screen and slowly reveal the graph, but it is too tempting to cheat.

4. Play a stockmarket game or simulation that is fun, realistic and helps you to get better.

Hence we developed Profit – the game that helps you practice.

A brief summary of the rules of the game is given below and in many ways these can be interpreted as rules of the market.

Running Profit

Having launched the program you can choose a stop-loss value of your choice, say, 15%. Then a level of play is offered which determines the speed at which graphs are scrolled in front of the player. The graphs may seem to be drawing fast at first, but in time you will find this to be slow. The player presses arrow keys for buying and selling while the graph draws from start to finish.

Your portfolio value, and changes, are shown in the bottom right hand corner of the screen. The prices at which you buy or sell are displayed to the left of this. The game runs for three minutes. The higher the level you choose, the faster the graphs will be drawn. This gives you more opportunity to increase (or decrease) the value of your portfolio. At the end of each game you are given a statistics box (you can print out the results), telling you which stocks you traded, how much you made, details on your winning and losing trades and overall rate of return. The tips for maximising the score in the game will be familiar to readers.

The main rules to buying and selling shares are:

1. **Cut Losses.**

2. **Cut Losses.**

3. **Cut Losses.**

4. **Let Profits Run.**

The way to do this is:

1. **To become skilled at spotting reversals in price movement.**

2. **Minimise losses on your losing trades.**

3. **Maximise profits on your winning trades.**

Always remember:

1. **You can sell a falling share and buy back at a cheaper price.**

2. **A few big winning trades can outweigh many small losers.**

The only technical tool we provide with the game is a stop-loss, as we believe this is critical for observing the essential rules.

Stop-loss

The best way to keep losses small and protect profits.

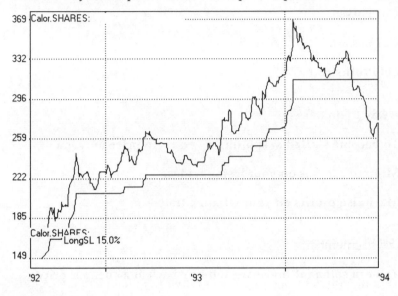

Source: Updata
Using Profit to 'let profits run... and run'.

The stop-loss is drawn as a selected percentage below the graph and only moves up when the graph moves above the previous high point. To use stop-loss effectively you must sell whenever the graph cuts down through the stop-loss. The stop-loss spends most of its time going horizontal which is proof that shares often spend more time going down than up.

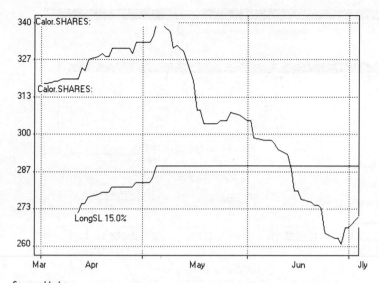

Source: Updata

Using Profit to 'cut losses quickly'.

Accepting you got it wrong, sooner rather than later can be the most valuable lesson in playing the market. Cut a loss and get back into a good position because 'time is money' – especially if your investments are falling in value. Take losses in your stride and buy back in at a cheaper price nearer the bottom.

At the end of each game the player is given the vital statistics. A sample of this is shown on page 92.

Updata Win results			☒
Summary of game number	1		

Company	+/- Change (£)	%Profit	
BODDING	402	5	▲
WADD'TON	4922	59	
KINGFISH	5241	50	
AB_PORTS	37933	151	
DOLPHIN	5112	18	
NTHN_EL	76478	105	
NEXT	1524443	1187	▼

	Number	Profit/Loss (£)	%ROI
Winning trades	18	2734204	26306
Losing trades	8	-103549	
Total trades	26	2630655	High Scores

Start	Quit	Settings	Help

Source: Updata

As I was writing, I took three minutes out to play a game of Profit. It is fair to say I have practiced quite a bit. The key is that although I have eight losing trades, my losses are small. This is because I used the stop-loss to cut them early. I had more winning trades and they were very profitable. Again I used the stop-loss to let my profits run until I saw a reversal of 15%. This may look like magic, but it's not.

We developed Profit so that people could prove it to themselves, that they really can make money in the stockmarket. What is great about it is that the more you play, the better you get. We are now starting to include it with our products so that people can practice regularly and keep an understanding of when to cut losses and sell. It is also proving to be a great tool for spotting reversals in price movement.

We believe this is an example of how future technology will help investors get better. Market simulations and interactive demonstrations or books will give people the kind of abilities that professionals with a long exposure to markets gain through experience.

The following series of graphs are snapshots throughout a game, with some brief explanations for my actions.

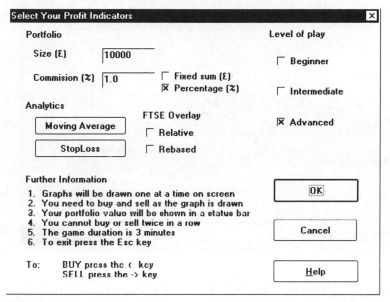

Source: Updata

A 15% stop-loss is fine for cutting losses and running with profits in the game.

Updata Profit v1.0
File Window Help

Sold @ 320p   £12494 +4646

Source: Updata

The stop-loss is drawn while I am in the stock. I got it wrong on my first trade in early 1992 thinking the shares were breaking out, but got out quickly. At the end of 1992 I felt the stock had turned around sufficiently to get back in and run with the rise until my stop-loss was breached.

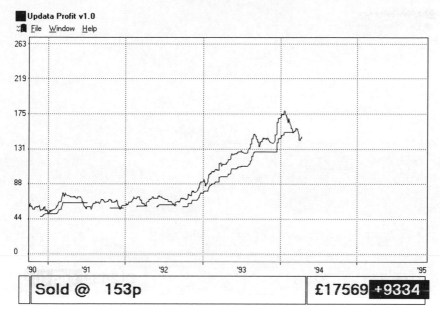

Updata Profit v1.0

File   Window   Help

Sold @   153p   £17569 +9334

Source: Updata

Again, it took me a few times to get it right taking a small loss each time, but my losses were outweighed when I was able to run with the profit.

Source: Updata

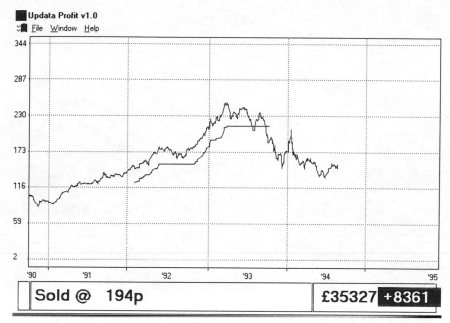

Updata Profit v1.0
File Window Help

Sold @ 194p	£35327 +8361

Source: Updata

It took me some time to identify that this stock was well behaved and trending. I got out before the stop-loss was breached because there was a second peak which wasn't as high as the one before it. From this I ascertained that the shares were beginning a downward trend.

*   *   *

CHAPTER NINE

Finding stocks to buy

• •

Most investors seem to have no problems finding stocks to buy. I worry that the selection process usually seems to be based on what they read in the press. You need to give yourself an edge and the press is unlikely to provide you with this. It is also very difficult to keep on top of all the information that may be written about a company. I have come across a few investors who have found clever ways of getting information on companies, but on the whole it is difficult. Information is often hidden in the graph, as covered in Chapter Twelve. Your overriding strategy should be to try and spot things before a larger audience does. Find a way of giving yourself an edge and specialise in one or two techniques.

Another point worth mentioning is that many private investors have developed a love affair with 'penny shares' in small companies which have a very low volume of trading in their shares. Over 95% of UK equity trading volume occurs in the top half of UK stocks. Efficiency of markets dictates that this higher volume will mean that the shares should behave more predictably. There is certainly money to be made in smaller companies but institutions are more busy trading in the bigger ones. Again I am concerned that many investors whom I meet buy these shares focused on the potential returns without assessing the risks. If you give someone the chance of one bet at a roulette table, they are more likely to go for the 35-1 shot than the opportunity to double their money. I have focused on graphs of large companies here as their behaviour is easier to predict. The rewards can also be very substantial. This optimises the risk versus return assessment that investors should make.

What to look for.

There are a number of criteria and here are a few:

1. Recovery situations – reversals from a long-term trend.

2. Breakouts –   dramatic movements from a narrowing trading range.

3. Trending stocks – shares already behaving in a clear upward trend.

4. Character changes – a change in behaviour.

Recovery Situations

Here, one is looking for a classic 'hockey stick' graph. A share has been in a long downward trend and then seems to rally, from what seems to be the floor. The best way to illustrate this is with some examples.

Source: Updata

Here Asda was in a long-term downward trend. The key characteristic in a downtrend is the graph moves sideways across the trend and then at the resistance level moves dramatically to the bottom of the trend channel. The reverse tends to be true in an uptrend. Asda's first sign of weakness was the peak in autumn 1989, which was lower than the previous peak. Again a downtrend will have descending peaks, an uptrend ascending.

Asda's shareholders shouldn't have been surprised to see the value of their shares keep falling. On the whole when a market plummets it doesn't bounce back. An exception to the rule is the Gorbechev coup which momentarily affected the Frankfurt index. I remember people predicting that sterling was a good buy after the ERM crisis, but in this instance there was no foreseeable end to the coup (see page 102).

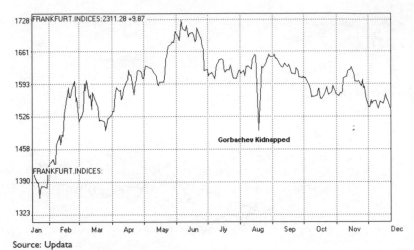

Source: Updata

The market recovered quickly because the crisis was over.

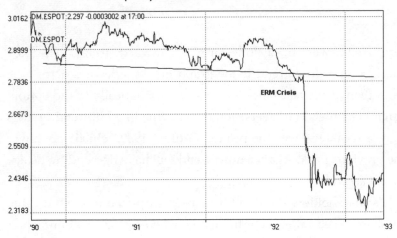

Source: Updata

The market didn't recover quickly because the crisis wasn't over.

Anyway back to Asda. In Autumn 1992, Asda shares broke out (see next section on Breakouts) and started trading in a tighter more predictable uptrend. Asda was showing the first signs of recovery. This shorter term uptrend started to falter as the shares approached the longer term resistance level. This should come as no surprise as the longer term trend normally wins. This was the most encouraging test of the downtrend resistance and the shares were already heading into new ground. The Asda graph then drifted sideways out into new territory and is now trading in a new uptrend. A couple of short-term uptrends within this longer term trend are shown. The following overlaid graphs give some idea of how far Asda may have to run. This shows how one can build knowledge very quickly.

Source: Updata

Asda rebased against FT-SE 100 index, shows the shares may still have some way to run.

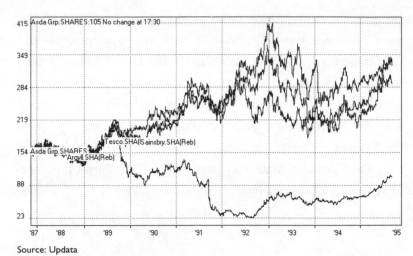

Source: Updata

Asda rebased against other companies in the stores sector, further emphasising the company's under-performance.

There are always a number of recovery stocks to look for; the graphs opposite show some that have recovered. You need to keep an eye on stocks that are in a downtrend with a view to spotting the breakout indicating recovery. All of these trend channels were drawn on using an auto-trend channel feature. This is based on the mathematical principle of regression analysis. While it isn't as accurate as drawing trendlines across peaks and troughs manually, it is great for identifying general trends.

Source: Updata

BP recovers, as did many stocks in autumn 1992.

Source: Updata

Blue Circle has a lot of lost ground to make up.

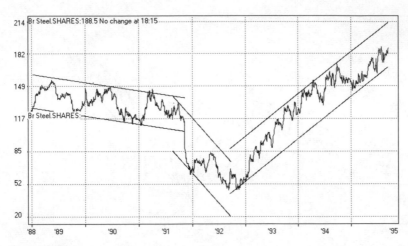

Source: Updata

British Steel - starts to recover in early 1993.

Source: Updata

British Aerospace also recovers in 1993.

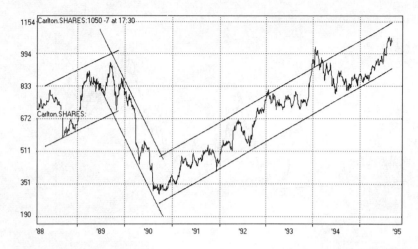

Source: Updata

Carlton - recovers in 1991.

Source: Updata

Forte's recovery was more difficult to spot, and has been fairly
weak after the initial run.

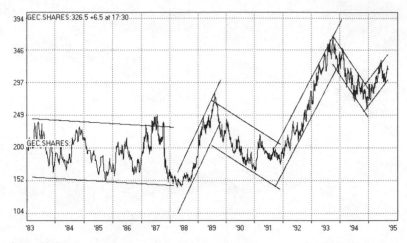

Source: Updata

GEC's recovery starts with a breakout at the end of 1991.

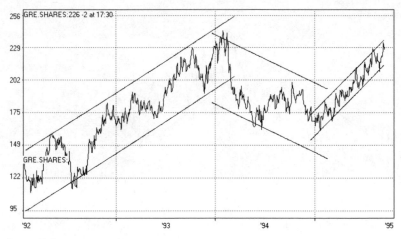

Source: Updata

Guardian Royal Insurance start trading in a more predictable
trend channel at the beginning of 1995.

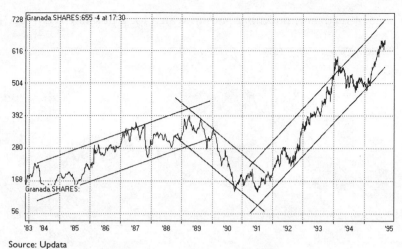

Source: Updata

Granada turns in 1991.

Source: Updata

Fisons finally turns around in 1995.

When I show this in a demonstration, it is normally at this point that people indicate that I have the benefit of hindsight. Let's try and identify some stocks that look as if they are about to recover. These are not predictions of recovery, but more ones to watch for a possible recovery.

Source: Updata

Enterprise Oil starting to trade sideways out of trend.

Source: Updata

Inchcape shows first signs of a trend after plummeting.

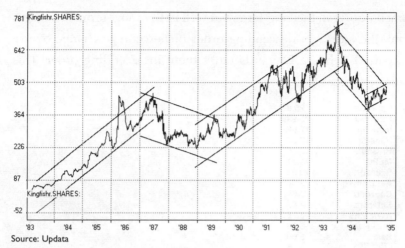

Source: Updata

Kingfisher, a new trend building, will it win this time?

Source: Updata

Ladbroke's are trading sideways for the first time in a while.

With so many stocks to choose from, finding buying opportunities can be time consuming. Carrying out what we call a Leaders and Laggards over different periods can help to spot stocks that have performed poorly in the long-term, but well in the short-term. A Leaders will rank the stocks in descending order of percentage change over a chosen period, while a Laggards ranks them in ascending order. This can indicate a breakout.

1	Caradon	-25.8
2	P&O dfd	-23.98
3	Inchcap	-17.62
4	Hanson	-12.83
5	Br Gas	-12.36
6	MEPC	-11.71
7	Schrodr	-10.53
8	Ald Domeq	-9.98
9	Courtald	-9.69
10	Enterprs	-7.69
11	AWiggins	-6.25
12	Scot Pwr	-5.73
13	Sears	-5.65
14	Kingfish	-1.8
15	Cable&W	-0.97
16	ICI	-0.71
17	DeLa Rue	-0.53
18	Grand Mt	0.24
19	Tate & L	0.78
20	Land Sec	0.82

Source: Updata

FT-SE 100 yearly Laggards, showing rank and percentage change.

1	Std Chtd	17.95
2	South El	16.85
3	BritAero	15.02
4	Scot Pwr	11.04
5	HSBC $	8.98
6	NatWest	8.55
7	Siebe	8.18
8	GEC	7.76
9	Barclays	7.18
10	ICI	6.97
11	DeLa Rue	6.89
12	Legal &G	6.61
13	Br Steel	6.5
14	Bnk Scot	6.3
15	NatPower	6.25
16	Sun All	6.07
17	SKlineB	5.6
18	ThornEMI	5.33
19	Br Air	5
20	Shell	4.61

Source: Updata

FT-SE 100 monthly Leaders, showing rank and percentage in a month.

Source: Updata

Are Scottish Power turning?

Scottish Power has fallen over 5% on the year and risen 11% in a month. Something must be happening, so I then double click on the price to look at the graph. This technique saves scrolling (even though you can scroll – hands free – and just sit back and watch) through many graphs to find potential recovery situations. The same can be done for breakouts. One looks for stocks that have near zero change in the yearly Laggards, but dramatic increases in the monthly Leaders.

Using Stop-loss as a 'Startprofit'

While working on a joint venture for futures trading in the US, we at Updata came across the ability to use stop-loss in reverse. Futures traders make the most of both rises and falls by going short. This is effectively selling at a high price and then buying it back at a lower price. Anyway using a short stop-loss is ideal for identifying when a stock has reversed by a certain percentage.

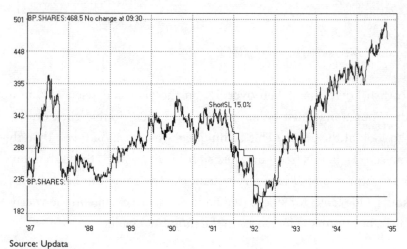

Source: Updata

BP – using a **short** stop-loss as a buy indicator.

Breakouts.

To spot breakouts we are looking for stocks that have traded sideways for a long time and have recently changed to a new gear. So the principles for finding stocks that are breaking out are similar to those used for recovery stocks. There should be little or no change over a year and a dramatic change over a month. Ideally the change over one year and one month should be the same. Four examples of breakout stocks are given on pages 115 and 116.

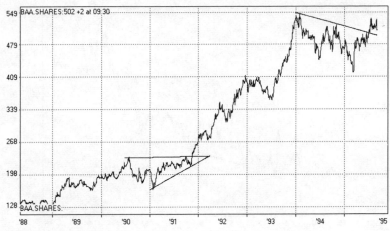

Source: Updata

BAA - slowdown then breakout, twice.

Source: Updata

Bank of Scotland, breaking into new territory again.

Source: Updata

Cable & Wireless – a new gear.

Source: Updata

NatWest – making up lost ground.

Trending Stocks

Trending Stocks

Most stocks don't behave in well defined trends for long periods of time, but here are a few that seem to go on and on.

Source: Updata

M & S – very well behaved.

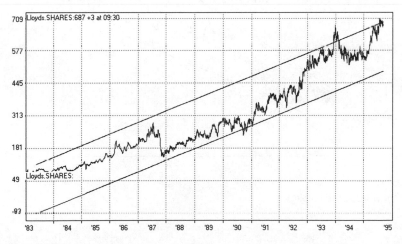

Source: Updata

Lloyds Bank – a tight trading range.

Source: Updata

Shell – no slippery slopes.

Source: Updata

Boots – now less predictable.

Source: Updata

Scottish & Newcastle is one of the best trending stocks there is,
great for worry free investment.

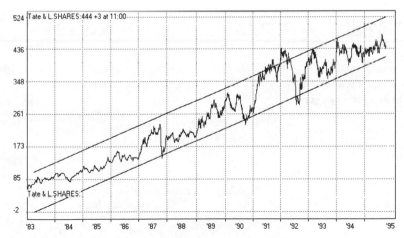

Source: Updata

Tate & Lyle are also well behaved.

Character Changes

Recoveries and breakouts are effectively character changes. The examples which follow show other instances where there is a fundamental change of behaviour. These are most easily spotted when graphs go from smooth to erratic behaviour, or vice versa.

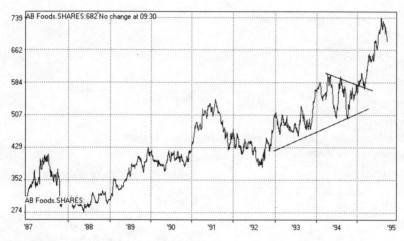

Source: Updata

AB Foods – experience big sudden falls in 1994, and sudden recoveries, twice, before running again.

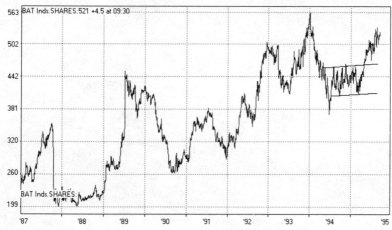

Source: Updata

BAT – this share has become progressively erratic in its short-term trading.
More jerky now than before.

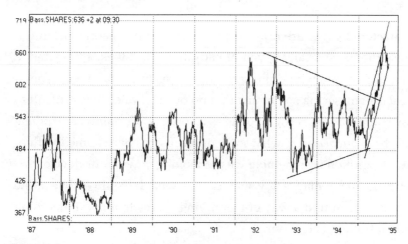

Source: Updata

Bass – trading in a short-term trend channel for the first time in years,
but could it now be heading back to its old ways?

Source: Updata

Thorn EMI – were already doing nicely over the long-term, but they have never traded in this tight trading range before.

Character changes are difficult to buy into, but it is often useful to recognise them, especially if you already hold the stock. I have met a number of investors who claim certain patterns never fail them. This is the great dream, seeing something that no one else does. It is difficult to say how valid pattern recognition is as a strategy. Certainly, at Updata, we have been surprised at what some of our users have claimed to find. Pattern recognition is something we are looking at with our developers, whereby the user may set visual parameters. It could prove quite exciting, if we can find a way of identifying shares that are undergoing changes in trading behaviour.

CHAPTER TEN

Monitoring

• •

Most people monitor their stocks by regularly looking at the prices in the newspaper. This is a bit like the Lottery. You have bought your stocks and now you hope they go up. If they start falling, you find it hard to accept a loss and you turn a blind eye to the losers and focus on your winners. Gamblers are very good at telling you about their winners. For every person who has told me where they lost money, dozens have told me where they made excellent profits.

Graphs are ideal for monitoring shares because they tell you how they are performing at a glance. Moreover graphs can also tell you very quickly that the picture may be changing.

Did you get it right?

So you have bought some shares and projected what you think may happen; your monitoring should now be quite rigid along these original ideas. There are a number of tools you can use for monitoring your shares. Trends and stop-loss are among the best. Stop-loss is very straightforward and has been covered earlier. Well behaved shares trade in clear trend channels. The question is how long will a trend carry on for and what are the signs that it is ending?

Support is the bottom line

The real key is to establish the trend you are following and the line of support for that trend. If it is a new trend developing, stop-loss will be more useful. As the trend matures, its form will become more clear and a rough line of support is something you need to become skilled at spotting. If you need to practice this, every time you see price graphs in the newspaper or a good investment magazine, draw support lines along the bottom of the trend.

When giving demonstrations, people often say 'Why did you draw that line there?' The easiest way to answer the question, is to do it again and again, until they see it for themselves.

If you are not good at spotting trends or trend channels, then an auto-trend channel facility in computer software is a good way of starting. This is also very useful for identifying where the price is in the trend as well as signs that a trend may be ending. Many examples of trend channels are shown in the previous chapter.

How to spot the end of the trend

The clearest sign that the trend is ending, is a breakdown through support. Examples of this have already been shown. There are some other signs to watch that may indicate the end of the trend. Volatility at the end of the trend and descending peaks are often good indications of a breakdown.

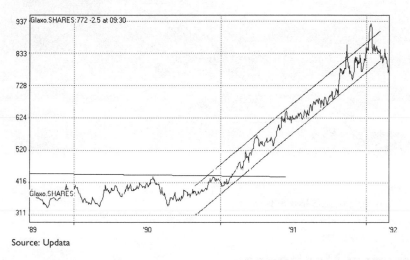

Source: Updata

Glaxo traded in a very tight trend channel for more than a year where it more than doubled. Towards the end of 1991, the shares started going haywire and broke through the top of the trend. This would normally be a good sign, but Glaxo's performance over the past year indicated that it was highly unlikely that an even steeper trend could be maintained. This is the time to be on guard. Volatility at the end of a steep trend is usually the first sign that the trend is coming to an end. Using stop-loss as shown on page 126 would have got you out as well. 10% was too early and 15% was a little late. On the whole stop-loss is easier to use, as there is no artistic interpretation as with trendlines. Playing the Updata Profit market simulation game is testament to this. Stop-loss is the easiest indicator to use for interpreting a reversal.

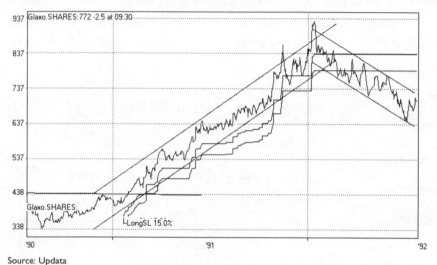

Source: Updata

Glaxo – showing the stop-loss indicators.

Numerical Monitoring

Most of us understand monitoring as looking up the price. It is surprising that many investors don't have a clear idea of the under and overperformers in their portfolios. This can be a chore to calculate on a frequent basis. Using a Leaders and Laggards facility gives an exact view of performance over a given period. It is also useful to include the FT-SE 100 or All Share index to see if you are out-performing the market.

1	BritAero	55.7		11	Br Steel	13.71
2	BSkyB	49.31		12	Abbey Nt	13.07
3	Asda Grp	40.07		13	FTSE	11.25
4	Amstrad	39.83		14	Br Air	11
5	ThornEMI	34.31		15	Scot Pwr	9.5
6	Vodafone	32.75		16	Glaxo	9.35
7	HSBC	28.92		17	BP	9.21
8	Barclays	19.1		18	Pearson	5.88
9	NatWest	18.2		19	M & S	3.84
10	3i	16.14		20	Sainsbury	2.11

Source: Updata

Sample portfolio – Leaders and Laggards.

Leaders and Laggards are ideal for looking at performance over a fixed time frame and the relative merits of each stock. Different shares perform better at different times and your portfolio should reflect that. In Chapter Five we looked at spreadsheets. The spreadsheet allows us to take numerical monitoring a step further by looking at the rate of return based on how long the shares have been held.

Example portfolio

Title	Price	Qnty	Value	BuyAt	BuyOn	Chg	Prof	%Prof	%ARR
SHARES									
3i	403	400	1,612	296	19-Jul-94	107	428	36	30
Abbey Nt	532	200	1,064	426	18-Dec-94	106	212	25	32
Amstrad	244	800	1,952	170	03-Mar-95	74	592	44	76
Asda	104	1,000	1,040	55	18-Feb-94	49	490	89	55
BP	468.5	500	2,343	229	26-Nov-92	240	1,198	105	37
BSkyB	380	500	1,900	254	22-Jan-95	126	630	50	72
Barclays	742	300	2,226	635	06-Apr-95	107	321	17	35
Br Air	454	250	1,135	395	12-Mar-95	59	148	15	27
Br Steel	182.5	500	913	74	04-Feb-93	109	543	147	55
BritAero	738	200	1,476	536	19-Jun-95	202	404	38	135
Glaxo	772	250	1,930	672	23-Feb-95	100	250	15	25
HSBC	887	150	1,331	752	26-Apr-95	135	203	18	42
M & S	433	400	1,732	254	10-Jul-91	179	716	70	17
NatWest	630	300	1,890	480	28-Aug-94	150	450	31	29
Pearson	594	300	1,782	603	20-Jun-95	-9	-27	-1	-5
Sainsbury	436	300	1,308	423	26-Mar-95	13	39	3	6
Scot Powr	351.5	400	1,406	340	31-Aug-95	12	46	3	43
Thorn EMI	1,472	200	2,944	1,171	25-Apr-95	301	602	26	60
Vodafone	263.5	500	1,318	220	08-Jun-95	44	218	20	64
Total			31,300			111	393	39	44

The spreadsheet also gives you the facility to view the performance
and breakdown of your portfolio at a glance as shown on page 129.

Portfolio Performance - Annualised Rate of Return

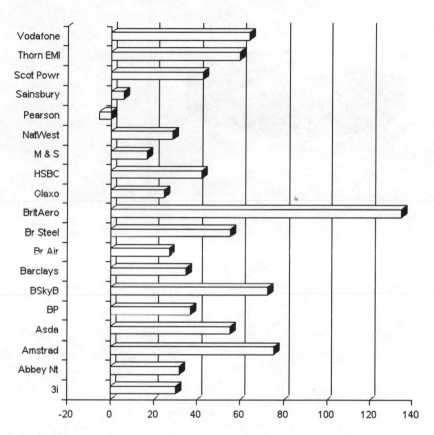

Source: Updata

Portfolio - Latest Breakdown

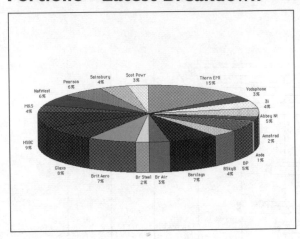

Source: Updata

CHAPTER ELEVEN

When to sell

* *

We have already identified in most of the previous chapters that this is the most important aspect to successful investment. Let's recap and look at the instances when one should sell.

Taking Profits - a reversal from the trend

This was partly covered in the previous chapter with the use of support levels and stop-loss. We also covered this under practising using the Profit game, where the key was to let profits run. Once support or the stop-loss is broken, especially in a long trend, then one shouldn't hesitate to sell. As a refresher on when to spot the end of a good run and time to sell, there are some examples on the next page. The time to sell is when the price line cuts through the other line shown.

Source: Updata

Forte – a sell in 1990, not a full recovery yet.

Source: Updata

Guinness – change direction to sideways in 1992.

Source: Updata

Hanson – looks like the end of this long run, in 1995.

Source: Updata

Inchcape – falls through two levels in 1994 and 1995.

Source: Updata

Kingfisher – a fall from grace 1993, 1994.

Source: Updata

Ladbroke's – two opportunities to get out, 1990 and 1992.

Source: Updata

Land Securities – two good runs end in 1989 and early 1994.

Source: Updata

MEPC – another two good runs end as with Land Securities.

Taking Losses

Taking profits is what everybody likes, but now we need to focus on the business of losses. Please remember the four main rules we covered in the Introduction.

1. Cut Losses.

2. Cut Losses.

3. Cut Losses.

4. Let Profits Run.

Shares that fall out of bed

There are two main instances where this applies. The more common one is where the shares you have just bought start to fall gradually but consistently. The other instance is where a share just falls out of bed, normally on the back of an announcement which surprises the market. We have already mentioned that downtrending stocks tend to move sideways across the channel and then fall sharply to the bottom of the channel. Therefore, as you shouldn't be in stocks that are in downtrends, this is less likely to happen to you. Do remember, however, on the whole shares that plummet rarely recover quickly. Examples of this were given in Chapter Nine; *Finding stocks to buy.* The Dmark and Frankfurt graphs were used. The main message in that instance was to deter investors from buying a share that has plummeted. It is unlikely to be considered cheap by the market and will not bounce back. The exception is some extraordinary circumstance such as a company's CEO being kidnapped. If you do pile in, you better hope he is found and are able to resume work the next day.

Recognising you got it wrong – early on

Good fund managers get it right six or seven times out of ten. The best ones make sure the few times they get it wrong, it is not expensive. The easiest way to recognise you got it wrong, is to write notes of your reasons for buying and what you expect to happen at the time. If you are lucky enough to have software that stores your analysis which also grows with the graph then you can monitor your positions more closely and spot a turnaround from your earlier predictions.

Having said all this, it is difficult with the benefit of hindsight, to show examples where the unexpected happened. We earlier identified that Asda had turned initially but realised once we saw it happening that the longer trend was still preventing it from rallying. Logically we can look at the instances we identified under shares to buy for what can go wrong:

1. A failed recovery.

2. A failed breakout.

3. Getting into a long trend which ends soon after.

4. Identifying a character change which leads to nothing.

An example of each of these is given on pages 138 and 139.

Source: Updata

Fisons – had hit the floor all right, but the recovery didn't come for more than a year, followed by a bid. The absence of a new trend building was a warning.

Source: Updata

Cadbury – broke out and ended up going the other way. A 10% stop-loss would have got you out before a further 15% deterioration.

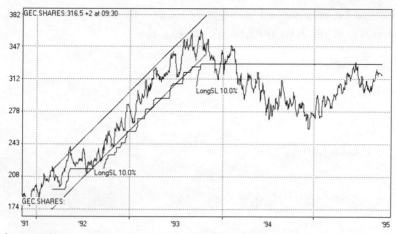

Source: Updata

GEC – in at the end of the trend, stop-loss would have got you out in the same manner, had you been in a year earlier - you were too late.

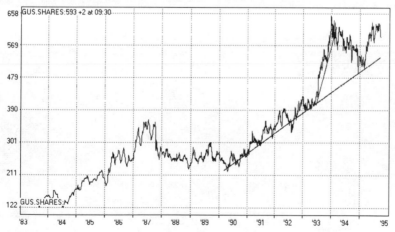

Source: Updata

GUS – a character change that was fairly short lived. Volatility came quite early in the trend and the shares reversed. You need to be quick.

It cannot be emphasised enough. Most private investors sell their good shares and sit on their bad ones. Remember:

1. Cut Losses.

2. Cut Losses.

3. Cut Losses.

4. Let Profits Run.

CHAPTER TWELVE

Getting more sophisticated

We have already covered a good deal that the majority of investors miss. I believe that short-term indicators are further than most investors need to go. I will only cover the most commonly used short-term technical indicators in this chapter. There are many more, which make things too technical for the purposes of this book.

Studying the graph more closely – spotting the gaps in the market

If you have the time or the inclination, there is still a lot more information hidden in the graph. From one five year price history, you can easily generate a thousand words. If the graph has high/low information on it then you can generate another thousand words as this adds another dimension. The high/low spikes and the gaps between them can provide a wealth of information as to what is going on. These gaps normally signal character changes as follows.

There are four main types of gap to look out for and these are best illustrated by examples.

1. Breakaway Gap.

2. Runaway Gap.

3. Exhaustion Gap.

4. Downside Breakaway Gap.

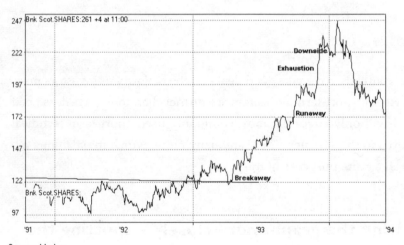

Source: Updata

This sequence of gaps is quite common with stocks that runaway. It is useful to know the stages, especially at the peak.

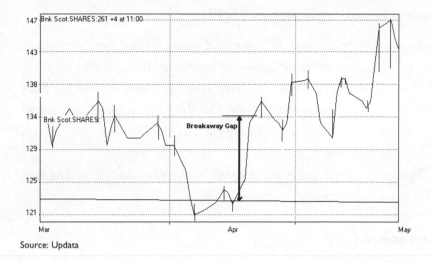

Source: Updata

The shares fall to the resistance level. Resistance often acts as a new support level and this confirmation, an unwillingness to enter old territory, is a good sign.

A gap is defined as when the high during a day is lower than the low the following day. This is a good indication of strength. The reverse situation is when the low is higher than the high the following day. Also, when the share closes at its high this shows strength especially if this happens for a number of days in a row. When it closes at its low this shows weakness. This is easy to spot as spikes pointing downward and spikes pointing upward respectively.

Short-Term Indicators (STI)

There are five main higher order indicators, which are sometimes referred to as short-term indicators or oscillators because they oscillate either side of a central horizontal axis. They are based on looking back over a relatively short period of time. The short descriptions that follow serve as a brief explanation of where each of them is derived from and how to interpret them.

The first two indicators are derived from using moving averages in the way we have already mentioned.

Momentum (MOM)

The momentum of a price line measures, as its name implies, whether the price line is running out of, or gathering, steam. This is where using cycle periods really pays off, because it is calculated as the ratio between the current price and the price of one full cycle ago.

In the example which follows on page 145, I am using the shares of BTR (top graph) with the Momentum indicators below.

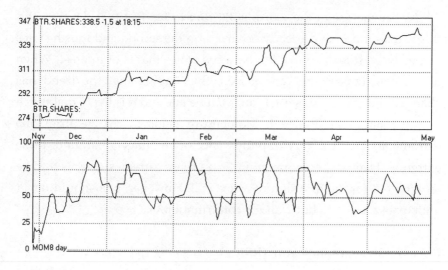

Source: Updata

BTR – Momentum indicators.

It is necessary to look back and see how the price line changed with previous signals. A quarter and a half cycle length often give good signals, but again it is a case of studying this in a historical context. We are looking for extremes in the graph.

Momentum is normally in one of four states;

1. Positive (ie. above the central axis) and rising; prices are increasing and accelerating (ie. they are increasing more and more quickly).

2. Positive and falling (ie. decelerating); prices are 'still' moving up, but more slowly.

3. Negative and falling; prices are falling more and more rapidly.

4. Negative and rising; prices are 'still' falling but less and less rapidly.

Notice the use of the word 'still', due to the fact that the first and third states must have already occurred, in the second and fourth states respectively. It is the transition between states that is of interest. When momentum crosses the central axis, this implies that the trend has changed direction. This signal can often be late and it is likely that much of the change has occurred. Momentum tends to change from one extreme to another very rapidly, and often 'lingers' around these extremes. Hence when momentum is on these extremes you need to be looking out for the first sign of a reversal. However, one should never anticipate a reversal, but wait for confirmation.

Relative Strength Indicator (RSI)

The Relative Strength Indicator is in essence a measure of short-term momentum, and shows whether the price line is speeding up or slowing down. It is calculated by comparing the average of the falls with the average of the rises within the defined period. It is measured on a percentage scale of 0 to 100. When the indicator is below 25 the investment is oversold and when it is above 75 it is overbought.

RSI assists in deciding 'when' the price line is overbought or oversold. It is effectively a measure of momentum. It is automatically drawn on a percentage scale.

1. The area between 0% and 25% represents oversold.

2. The area between 75% and 100% represents overbought.

These regions are usually considered critical. Once again, this should be verified historically and adjusted accordingly as the areas actually are not so rigidly defined. These areas may also change slightly depending on the sort of market conditions that reign generally. For instance, in a bull market 80 and 30 may be the levels used, while in a bear market 70 and 20 may be more suitable. When the RSI starts to move out of these areas the signal to buy or sell is given. Hence when RSI is in the extreme bands one should anticipate when it is about to move into the central band. The RSI, unlike most other indicators, also works quite well in a sideways market, ie. where the trend channel points sideways.

Another consideration, often known as the 'divergence factor', is when the price line and the RSI are doing different things.

1. A price line scaling new peaks, when the RSI is not, is a bad sign and usually indicates that it is time to sell.

2. When a price line is at new lows, while the RSI is not, is a good sign and usually indicates that it is time to buy.

Overbought/Oversold (OBOS)

This is simply measured by the distance between the price line and its average. It is an extremely useful indicator as it tells the investor whether something is 'overbought' or 'oversold'. The OBOS line represents the price distance and appears often in a cyclical form due to the fact that the average oscillates about the price line. The main points of interest on the graph are the extremes where it starts to turn and especially where it crosses the zero axis which shows the price line is being crossed. This means that a price reversal may be imminent.

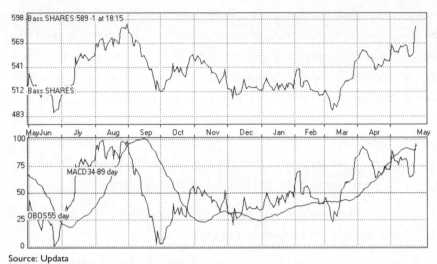

Source: Updata

Bass – using the OBOS and MACD indicators.

The OBOS is telling us information about the moving average technique without actually using it. It must be stressed that, the OBOS falling does not necessarily indicate that the price line is falling.

1. When the OBOS crosses the central axis we know that the moving average crosses the price line.

2. When the OBOS is near the extremes of the bottom window it is said to be 'overbought' (if near the top) or 'oversold' (near the bottom).

Study what the OBOS has done in the past in order to assess how extreme it actually is. If the OBOS is on or near its maximum distance away from the centre line then it is almost certain that this extreme cannot be sustained for very long at all. It is most likely that the price line will come back in line with its average. So, we should be looking for the

OBOS either 'topping out' in the overbought area or 'bottoming out' in the oversold area with a reversal in the other direction beginning to occur.

Moving Average Convergence/Divergence (MACD)

This graph comes from the second method of using moving averages. It measures the distance between two averages of different periods and is again used to spot divergence. It is similar to the overbought/oversold indicator in appearance and is also drawn on the same type of scale, as shown on page 148. Again, when this graph crosses the zero axis a 'buy' or 'sell' signal is given.

Like the OBOS, the MACD shows the distance between two lines (this time two moving averages) which is not always readily apparent just by looking at them. Use a full cycle period as the averaging length of the first moving average and a shorter period for the second.

- When the MACD crosses the central axis this means that the two moving averages are crossing each other and either a 'golden cross' or a 'dead cross' is occurring.

Stochastics

The last of the short-term indicators is a group of functions called the stochastics. These are sometimes used in probability and statistics. They assume that prices on the price line accumulate near the peaks of uptrends and the troughs of downtrends as does the data near the reversal points in a cycle. Therefore for this analysis to be effective the price history should follow a clear cycle. Like the other short-term indicators, these functions employ cycle periods. Basically the main stochastic function relates the current price to its relative position within the averaging period chosen. This function can then be averaged to produce lines much the same as in averages. 'Buy' and 'Sell' signals are given by these graphs in a similar manner to the analysis which uses moving averages of different averaging periods.

The main stochastic function relates the current price to its relative position within the averaging period. Another two graphs are automatically drawn with the stochastic graph. The first is a three day moving average of the stochastic, known as a K curve. The second is a three day moving average of the K curve, known as a D curve. These act as a smoothing measure and, as the averaging period implies, are best for short-term trading.

A simple analysis is as follows:

1. 'Bullish' divergence occurs where the price line falls to new lows while K moves upwards. The decision to buy is given when the K curve moves up through the stochastic line.

2. 'Bearish divergence' is where the price line reaches new peaks but the K curve does not. The sell signal is given on the day the K curve crosses down through the stochastic line.

After a strong rise or fall the price line often consolidates, away from the extreme values. Once the stochastics start moving in the opposite directions, a price reversal is imminent. Stochastics also show overbought and oversold at the extremes.

The 'double smoothing' effect of the D curve can be utilised to avoid 'whiplash' effects removing erratic fluctuations present in the analysis using the stochastic curve and K. The analysis is the same except K now takes the place of the stochastic curve and D takes the place of K.

Basically buy signals are given when K rises above D and sell signals when K moves below D.

Stochastics can be useful for short-term trading in the trend channel. The price line often turns before or after the boundaries and stochastics can show this clearly.

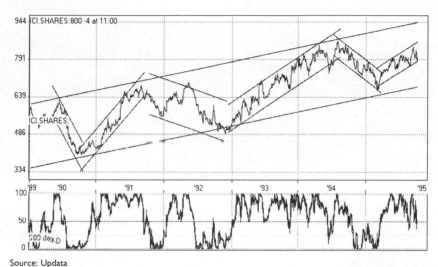

Source: Updata

ICI – stochastic graph.

The dramatic moves in the stochastic from one extreme to the other match ICI's moves across the trend. It also oscillates in the top or bottom half for the secondary trend. This graph above shows a lot more clearly what is going on.

CHAPTER THIRTEEN

Some examples of a regular routine

The frequency of your routine will vary according to the term of your investments. There are no hard and fast rules and routines often get broken. I would suggest that the time frames below are appropriate. I would also recommend that you don't skip more than one of these time frames. The key is to let a computer do a lot of the work for you so that watching your investments is much more enjoyable.

Short-Term Investor – hold for days, weeks – daily routine.

Medium-Term Investor – hold for weeks, months – weekly routine.

Long-Term Investor – hold for months, years – monthly routine.

A Structured Analysis Routine

1. Analyse the market first. Get a feel for the direction of the market and keep it in mind through the rest of the analysis. The following steps can be carried out for the market index and then for the particular investment required. Make a note of the latest support level and where it will be next time you analyse it. UK investors should also do this for the Dow Jones. If the market falls sharply below these levels, you may need to act quickly. Certainly be prepared to analyse everything again at this point to re-evaluate your position.

2. The first thing when looking at any price line is to try and spot a trend. Trends are the single most important indicator. If a trend cannot be determined, it is really very questionable whether the rest of the analysis should proceed. 'The trend is your friend'.

3. Once trends are established try and identify the likely direction of the price line in the short-term.

    a) If it has just bounced off resistance or support then it will be towards the other extreme. Determine the price level of this extreme.

    b) The best signal is given by a breakout where a trendline has clearly been breached. The price line is moving into new territory.

Certainly, when support is clearly broken you should sell. If you want to cover many price lines in a short time, then look for trends and patterns only. Use stop-loss for monitoring. Having done this for the market, you can now do it for each of your shares. If you want to get more technical you can proceed with the following steps.

4. Try and identify cycles. The main reason for this is to estimate period lengths of the price line.

5. Use overlays to compare the price line with other price lines. The most powerful method is to use the relative overlay with the relevant index. Look for potential price re-ratings.

6. Use moving averages of the period estimated on the price line and look at intersections between them. If the chosen period has not given clear signals in the past try adjacent Fibonacci numbers until you get clear signals. Now look at what the price line has done historically with each signal. This is the procedure for any indicator that uses periods.

7. Use two moving averages preferably of the two periods you have identified. Look for 'crosses'. If no clear signals try Fibonacci numbers.

8. Once you feel you can visualise step 6, try using the OBOS. Be prepared to go back and draw your interpretation using the moving average.

9. Step 7 can be replaced by using the MACD when you feel you have mastered it. Checking signals using the two moving averages is highly recommended.

10. Look at momentum and get a feel for whether the price line is running out of steam or gathering pace.

11. The RSI will tell you how strong a price line is relative to the period length selected. Again you are looking for this indicator being in overbought or oversold regions. Remember to compare the RSI to price line behaviour looking for previous confirmation of signals.

12. If a price line is beautifully cyclical try using the stochastic function.

Consult the correct interpretations of the indicator being used, including short lists of buy and sell signals, whenever you are in any doubt.

What not to do

The most important point is not to be guided by your emotions, especially fear and greed.

1. Don't decide on whether to buy, sell, or hold until you have completed the analysis, otherwise it will only confirm what you feel.

2. Don't be afraid to accept that you cannot determine what will happen. When in doubt do nothing if you are out. If you are in and in doubt, get out.

3. Adhere to the stop-loss rigidly. Protect profits by moving stop-loss up with rises. Protect against losses such that if you are down from the beginning cut your loss and get out.

4. Don't feel you have to trade. Wait for the best signals to come along.

5. Don't predict too far ahead. The further ahead you look the less accurate your prediction is likely to be.

6. Don't anticipate price reversals and breakouts. Wait for the signal to occur.

There are two Wall Street adages:

1. 'The majority is usually wrong'.

2. 'If it is obvious, it is obviously wrong'.

CHAPTER FOURTEEN

Conclusion

The last chapter covered the do's and don'ts in carrying out your analysis. This brief summary offers some more general guidance.

A few simple rules

There are many books on trading strategy available. A few fundamental rules are listed below.

1. Conserve capital at all costs. Never place more than 10% in any one trade.

2. Never act solely on advice.

3. Ignore impending dividends. Never hold or buy solely to collect a coming dividend.

4. **CUT LOSSES.** This is the most important rule. Adhere to stop-losses rigidly. Charting is a mechanical practice, there is no room for emotions or gut feelings. It will be impossible to get it right every time.

5. Let profits run. Wait for trends to be clearly broken. The trend is your friend.

At the very least using charting techniques should ensure no major investment mistakes are made.

If you don't have a computer already, you will have one sooner or later. They are likely to infiltrate our lives as the telephone has. The longer you leave it the harder you will find it to get on board. Get some software that will take care of data collection and helping you buy and sell.

True understanding comes through explanation. Put yourself to this test. Sit down with someone who has a mutual interest. This could be a friend at an investment club, a letter or fax to your broker, or a presentation to your husband or wife. Show them graphs of your shares and ones you are about to buy. If you have software to help you do this on screen, all the better. Now explain your actions as simply as possible. Then try and get this person to give you a brief summary of your explanation. Writing this book has really helped me clarify a number of points in my own mind. I hope it helps you to do something similar.

APPENDIX ONE

Internet Information addresses

• •

Financial Internet Directory

The pace of change on the Internet is probably unmatched in the history of mankind. This makes compiling a comprehensive and accurate directory fairly difficult. With companies setting up shop on the net every day, I am bound to have missed something that is already there and a lot more to come. To keep on top of this, you need to buy monthly magazines on the Internet or spend time looking around (surfing) on the net.

The list could be a good deal longer, but I have tried to keep it to the most relevant addresses. Many of these sites will have references or links to other related sites. Some are actually primarily a related sites index. It must be remembered the Internet knows no boundaries. Therefore, many of the entries offer information on other world markets. The sites are grouped under country. In order to get onto the site, you must enter the URL (Uniform Resource Locator) exactly as it is printed. Entries have the following format:

Name of site
Internet Address
Brief description where possible

United Kingdom

Brokers
http://www.cs.cmu.edu/afs/cs.cmu.edu/user/jdg/www/invest brokers.html

Charles Stanley
http://www.charles-stanley.co.uk/
CS Broking Services, on-line share prices proposed

The Economist
http://www.economist.com/

ESI
http://www.esi.co.uk/
Joint venture with UK broker, ShareLink, prices and on-line dealing

Financial Times
http://www.ft.com
News

HM Treasury

http://www.hm-treasury.co.uk/

News releases, budgets, ministers' speeches

InvestNet

http://www.mkn.co.uk/

On-line portfolio valuation, trading planned

Liffe

http://www.liffe.com/

One of the biggest sites, prices, news, courses, price histories

MoneyWeb

http://www.demon.co.uk/moneyweb/

Glossary of UK investments

MoneyWorld

http://www.moneyworld.co.uk

News, glossary, reviews, on-line publication

On-line IFAs Limited

http://www.onlineifa.co.uk/online/

Advice on pensions, PEPS, life assurance, trusts, etc

Optimum Technology

http://www.opt.com/opt

Software news, support, user group, prices, product literature

Telegraph

http://www.telegraph.co.uk/

Probably the most read sites in Britain, electronic newspaper

Updata

http://www.demon.co.uk/updata

Software news, support, user group, prices, product literature

United States

Aufhauser & Company's Wealth WEB

http://www.aufhauser.com

On-line brokerage, quotes and trading

Amex

http://www.amex.com

Dow Jones every 30 seconds, S&P 15 minute delay

Chicago Board Options Exchange

http://www.cboe.com

User friendly site, free video explaining instruments

Chicago Board Of Trade

http://www.cbot.com

User friendly as well as futures information

Chicago Mercantile Exchange

http://www.interaccess.com/cme

Off-line ticker – daily settlement and intra-day currencies

Etrade

http://www.etrade.com/etrade/html/ethome.htm

A well established site from this discount broker

FAST Broker

http://info.broker.isi.edu/1/fast

Prototype automated procurement service

Finance and Investment Virtual Office

http://www.virtual.office.com/finance/

Links to financial information on the web

FinWeb

http://www.finweb.com

University of Texas, financial sites index

Investment and Personal Finance

http://gnn.com/

Holt Report

http://turnpike.net.metro/holt/index.html

Daily summary of world indices, link to NYSE quote server –
15 minute delay

Lombard

http://www.lombard.com/

US Broker – 15 minute delayed quotes

MIT Artificial Intelligence Lab

http://www.mit.edu/stocks

A well known site providing experimental stock data – great

PAWWS Financial Network

http://www.pawws.secapl.com/top.html

Real time prices for AMEX, NASDAQ, NYSE – to subscribers $50 per month

QuoteCom

http://www.quote.com

Stock prices newsfeeds, etc – very popular site

Web Com Investors Galleria

http://www.webcom.com/galleria

Financial services, mailing list service and other services – image rich

Weekly Market Summary

http://www.gruntal.com/investments/wms.html

Summary which is useful for a weekly log on

Yahoo

http://www.yahoo.com/

Up-to-the-minute Reuters news

Continental and Eastern Europe

Amsterdam

http://www.aeb.econ.vu.nl

AEX Index real time, delayed stock information

Frankfurt

http://www.odin.csn.tu-chem-nitz.de:9999/ARD/422/1.

Good effort from German Teletext providers ARD/ZDF

Moscow - Russian Raw Commodity Exchange

http://www.fe.msk.ru/infomarket/rtsb/ewelcome.html

Basic and in Russian – but worth a look

Other Russian Financial Markets

http://mail.eskimo.com:80/bwest/finance.html

SASI Stock Market Analysis

http://www.europa.com/sasi/

Warsaw

http://info.fuw.edu.pl/pl/gielda.eng.html

Basic as it comes - pure data

Zagreb

http://ksaver208.zse.com.hr/

In-depth daily coverage and listed securities

Rest of the World

Australian Stock Exchange

http://www.asx.com.au

Regional directory of brokers, open days, investment courses, etc

Hong Kong

http://www.asia-inc.com/lippo/index.html

Hang Seng details, close prices and commentary of other Asian markets

Johannesburg Exchange

http://www.africa.com/pages/jse/page1.html

Searchable company information, spot rates, unit trusts, FOREX

Joburg Investor Web

http://www.investorweb.com

Range of financial sources

APPENDIX TWO

More Titles from Rushmere Wynne

● ●

Rushmere Wynne specialises in the publication of financial and investment books. Its current list includes the following titles:

THE PROSHARE GUIDE TO YOU AND YOUR STOCKBROKER
by John Cobb
(1993: Price £9.95 Paperback) ISBN 0–948035–03–X.
This book explains how to choose a stockbroker who can meet your own special needs.

THE INVESTORS' HANDBOOK
by Maggie Drummond
(1994: Price £6.95 Paperback) ISBN 0–948035–04–8.
An excellent introduction to the basics of stockmarket trading.

THE SECOND FINANCIAL SERVICES REVOLUTION
by Brian Tora
(1994: £12.95 Hardback) ISBN 0–948035–10–2.
For the investor who wants to understand what is happening in the revolution of the world of financial services, this book is a must.

THE PRIVATE INVESTOR'S
GUIDE TO THE STOCKMARKET
by Neil Stapley
(1994: Price £8.95 Paperback) ISBN 0–948035–11–0.
One of the best introductions to the stockmarket yet written by a leading private client stockbroker. The book explains how to build your share portfolio, how to evaluate shares, how to assess risk and much much more.

HOW TO MAKE A KILLING IN THE
ALTERNATIVE INVESTMENT MARKET
by Michael Walters
(1995: £9.95 Paperback) ISBN 0–948035–14–5.
The deputy City editor of the *Daily Mail*, Michael Walters, writes the third in his best selling trilogy of books for his numerous readers.

TRADED OPTIONS – A PRIVATE INVESTOR'S GUIDE:
how to invest more profitably
by Peter Temple
(1995: Price £16.95 Hardback) ISBN 0–948035–06–4
Written by the author and journalist, Peter Temple, the book explains traded options in a step-by-step style. It is sponsored by LIFFE and ProShare.

EVERY WOMAN'S GUIDE TO PERSONAL FINANCE
by Rosanna Spero
(1995: Price £9.99 Paperback) ISBN 0–948035–15–3
Daily Mail journalist Rosanna Spero provides a practical guide for women of all ages and stages in the management of their finances.

INVESTMENT CLUBS:
The low-risk way to stockmarket profits.
by Tony Drury
(1995: Price £6.99 Paperback) ISBN 0–948035–22–6
Would you like to become a successful stockmarket investor? You can, by reading this book. Experience the fun and fellowship of investing in a low-risk way, within the confines of an investment club.

HOW TO MAKE A KILLING IN PENNY SHARES
by Michael Walters
(1995: Price £9.99 Paperback) ISBN 0–948035–20–X
Already sold 50,000, this is the updated version of the best seller written by the deputy City editor of the *Daily Mail*, Michael Walters.

PROFIT OF THE PLUNGE
by Simon Cawkwell
(1995: Price £9.99 Paperback) ISBN 0–948035–17–X
This book was banned by the judge in the Maxwell trial. Now available, it tells the secrets of one of the most active short-sellers of all time including his dealings with the Maxwell Communication Corporation. If you are interested in the stockmarket, this book is a 'must'.

CHARTERS ON CHARTING:
how to improve your stockmarket decision making.
by David Charters(1995: £12.95 Hardback) ISBN 0–948035–21–8
Already on its third reprint, this book has become a classic. It explains
how charting works. Described by *the Investors' book club* as "the best
charting book for the private investor we have seen."

JEFF'S LUNCHBOX
by Jeff Prestridge
(1995: £6.99 Paperback) ISBN 0–948035–27-7
This is the book the financial services industry has always feared would
be published. By putting together his lunch reports published in the
weekly trade paper *Investment Adviser,* together with revealing extracts
from his diary, Jeff Prestridge exposes the inside story of his industry.

All these books are available from leading bookshops or by writing to:

> **Rushmere Wynne Limited:**
> 4-5 Harmill,
> Grovebury Road,
> Leighton Buzzard,
> Bedfordshire LU7 8FF
> **Telephone: 01525 853726**
> **Fax: 01525 852037**

INDEX

Profit
for Windows

upData *software*

Profit, Updata's stockmarket simulation game covered in chapter 8, is free to all ***Profit from your PC*** readers.

Simply send this voucher, with your name, postal address and daytime telephone number to:

Updata Software Ltd
Updata House
Old York Road
London
SW18 1TG

Fax 0181 874 3931